T5-CUN-282

HOPE 1:8

MISSIONSCO-OP

"But you will receive power when the Holy Spirit comes on you; and you will be my witnesses in Jerusalem, and in all of Judea and Samaria, and to the ends of the earth."

Acts 1:8

COOPERATIVELY DOING MISSIONS

Consider Your Personal Answers To The Following Ministry Questions:

How many people did you feed last year?

How many churches did you start last year?

How many people did you lead to Christ last year?

Working Together:

By participating in a missions co-op, an individual or church is able to reach farther and do more in the name of Christ than any one person or church can do alone.

The Cooperative Program of the Baptist General Convention of Texas is a collective funding system that exists to carry out missions on a large scale. Just as one Christian alone cannot accomplish God's mandate to reach the world, neither can one church do all that is asked of a body of believers. The task before us demands cooperation.

Your gift to missions through the Cooperative Program allows individuals and churches to be involved actively in missions, evangelism, education, discipleship and human care in Texas and around the world.

The money you give feeds the hungry, starts churches, funds missionaries and mission projects.

The Cooperative Program Funds:

- » provide scholarships for ministerial students,
- » reach people in prison,
- » take a message of hope to the hopeless,
- » provide chaplains in Texas hospitals,
- » clothe the needy and so much more.

SPREADING HOPE

Each Tuesday during the semester, Lauren Sierra, campus missionary for the Sam Houston State University Baptist Student Ministry, walks to the center of campus where student activities are buzzing, taking with her two metal folding chairs and a white board that reads, "Take a seat – questions about life."

As hundreds of students passed by on their way to class, Laura sits for a few hours, leaving the second chair open for anyone who wants to sit and talk about life. Many students walk by, avoiding eye contact and heading to the other side of the walkway to avoid the chairs. But Sierra sits patiently, knowing that God will bring the people who need to hear hope and need a friend to listen.

"One thing I like about the 'Take a Seat' method is that they can come sit down if they want," Sierra says. "I'm not forcing anyone to come sit down with me. One of the first things that I say is that at any point in this conversation you are free to get up and go. You won't offend me. I'm just here to learn about your life and share my life with you."

" I've had students tell me they have a nature of darkness in them. Good thing is that Jesus is the light so I'm able to share the gospel with them. "

SPREADING HOPE CONT.

When students sit in the chair, Sierra begins asking general questions about their major, what they think the purpose of life is or if they follow a religion, questions that help get a conversation started. Then she listens, looking for ways to share the hope of Christ with each student.

"I've had students tell me they are bent towards sin," Sierra says. "I've had students tell me they have a nature of darkness in them. Good thing is that Jesus is the light so I'm able to share the gospel with them."

Sierra feels like this ministry and other BSM ministries are reaching the campus because they are fulfilling a need for community that many students have. In the process, Sierra brought other BSM students with her to teach them how they too can give a listening ear and a kind and truthful word to other students.

Gifts through the Texas Baptist Cooperative Program help support Baptist Student Ministries that are seeking to share the gospel with students on 118 Texas college campuses.

"When we talk about meeting needs, I think one of the biggest needs we need to meet on this campus is community," Sierra says. "People need someone to talk to, and I'm trying to provide that for them and share the gospel while doing it."

To find out how this money supports various mission aspects, visit texasbaptists.org/cp. Thank you for giving to missions through the Texas Baptist Cooperative Program.

TEXAS ★ BAPTISTS
BAPTIST GENERAL CONVENTION OF TEXAS

www.texasbaptists.org

333 N. Washington I Dallas, TX 75246-1798 I 888.244.9400

BAPTISTWAY ADULT BIBLE STUDY GUIDE®
LARGE PRINT EDITION

The Gospel of John

LIGHT OVERCOMING DARKNESS
PART TWO—THE LIGHT OVERCOMES (JOHN 13—21)

PHIL LINEBERGER
GARY LONG
RANDEL EVERETT
BILL SHIELL

BAPTISTWAYPRESS®
Dallas, Texas

The Gospel of John: Light Overcoming Darkness, Part Two—The Light Overcomes (John 13—21)—BaptistWay Adult Bible Study Guide®—Large Print

Copyright © 2011 by BAPTISTWAY PRESS®.
All rights reserved.
Printed in the United States of America.

No part of this book may be used or reproduced in any manner whatsoever without written permission except in the case of brief quotations. For information, contact BAPTISTWAY PRESS, Baptist General Convention of Texas, 333 North Washington, Dallas, TX 75246–1798.

BAPTISTWAY PRESS® is registered in U.S. Patent and Trademark Office.

Scripture marked NIV is taken from The Holy Bible, New International Version (North American Edition), copyright © 1973, 1978, 1984 by the International Bible Society. Used by permission of Zondervan Publishing House. Unless otherwise indicated, all Scripture quotations in lessons 1–3 and 8–11 are from the New International Version.

Scripture marked NRSV is taken from the New Revised Standard Version Bible, copyright 1989, Division of Christian Education of the National Council of the Churches of Christ in the United States of America. Used by permission. All rights reserved. Unless otherwise indicated, all Scripture quotations on the back cover, in "Introducing the Gospel of John: Light Overcoming Darkness, Part Two— The Light Overcomes (John 13—21)," and in lessons 4–5 are from the New Revised Standard Version Bible.

Scripture marked NASB is taken from the 1995 update of the New American Standard Bible®, Copyright © The Lockman Foundation 1960, 1962, 1963, 1968, 1971, 1972, 1973, 1975, 1977, 1995. Used by permission. Unless otherwise indicated, all Scripture quotations in lessons 6–7 are from the New American Standard Bible.

BAPTISTWAY PRESS® Leadership Team
Executive Director, Baptist General Convention of Texas: Randel Everett
Director, Education/Discipleship Center: Chris Liebrum
Director, Bible Study/Discipleship Team: Phil Miller
Publisher, BAPTISTWAY PRESS®: Ross West

Cover and Interior Design and Production: Desktop Miracles, Inc.
Printing: Data Reproductions Corporation

First edition: March 2011

ISBN–13: 978–1–934731–67–3

How to Make the Best Use of This Issue

Whether you're the teacher or a student—

1. Start early in the week before your class meets.

2. Overview the study. Review the table of contents and read the study introduction. Try to see how each lesson relates to the overall study.

3. Use your Bible to read and consider prayerfully the Scripture passages for the lesson. (You'll see that each writer has chosen a favorite translation for the lessons in this issue. You're free to use the Bible translation you prefer and compare it with the translation chosen for that unit, of course.)

4. After reading all the Scripture passages in your Bible, then read the writer's comments. The comments are intended to be an aid to your study of the Bible.

5. Read the small articles—"sidebars"—in each lesson. They are intended to provide additional, enrichment information and inspiration and to encourage thought and application.

6. Try to answer for yourself the questions included in each lesson. They're intended to encourage further thought and application, and they can also be used in the class session itself.

If you're the teacher—

A. Do all of the things just mentioned, of course. As you begin the study with your class, be sure to find a way to help your class know the date on which each lesson will be studied. You might do this in one or more of the following ways:

- In the first session of the study, briefly overview the study by identifying with your class the date on which each lesson will be studied. Lead your class to write the date in the table of contents on page 9 and on the first page of each lesson.

- Make and post a chart that indicates the date on which each lesson will be studied.

- If all of your class has e-mail, send them an e-mail with the dates the lessons will be studied.

- Provide a bookmark with the lesson dates. You may want to include information about your church and then use the bookmark as an outreach tool, too. A model for a bookmark can be downloaded from www.baptistwaypress.org on the Resources for Adults page.

- Develop a sticker with the lesson dates, and place it on the table of contents or on the back cover.

B. Get a copy of the *Teaching Guide*, a companion piece to this *Study Guide*. The *Teaching Guide* contains additional Bible comments plus two teaching plans. The teaching plans in the *Teaching Guide* are intended to provide practical, easy-to-use teaching suggestions that will work in your class.

C. After you've studied the Bible passage, the lesson comments, and other material, use the teaching suggestions in the *Teaching Guide* to help you develop your plan for leading your class in studying each lesson.

D. Teaching resource items for use as handouts are available free at www.baptistwaypress.org.

E. You may want to get the additional adult Bible study comments—*Adult Online Bible Commentary*—by Dr. Jim Denison (president, The Center for Informed Faith, and theologian-in-residence, Baptist General Convention of Texas). Call 1–866–249–1799 or e-mail baptistway@texasbaptists.org to order *Adult Online Bible Commentary*. It is available only in electronic format (PDF) from our website. See our website, www.baptistwaypress.org, for the price of these comments both for individuals and for a group. A church or class that participates in our advance order program for free shipping can receive *Adult Online Bible Commentary* free. Call 1–866–249–1799 or see www.baptistwaypress.org for information on participating in our free shipping program for the next study.

F. An additional teaching plan is also available in electronic format (PDF) by calling 1–866–249–1799. See our website, www.baptistwaypress.org, for the price of this item both for individuals and for a group. A church or class that participates in our advance order program for free shipping can receive *Adult Online Teaching Plans* free. Call 1–866–249–1799 or see www.baptistwaypress.org for information on participating in our free shipping program for the next study.

G. You also may want to get the enrichment teaching help that is provided on the internet by the *Baptist Standard* at www.baptiststandard.com. (Other class participants may find this information helpful, too.) Call 214–630–4571 to begin your subscription to the printed or electronic edition of the *Baptist Standard*.

H. Enjoy leading your class in discovering the meaning of the Scripture passages and in applying these passages to their lives.

Writers of This Study Guide

Phil Lineberger, writer of lessons one through three, is pastor of Sugar Land Baptist Church, Sugar Land, Texas. The church recently changed its name from Williams Trace Baptist Church to Sugar Land Baptist Church. Phil is married to Brenda, with three daughters and nine grandchildren. He has served as president of the Baptist General Convention of Texas, as a trustee for William Jewell College and Dallas Baptist University, as a regent at Baylor University, and as vice-president of the Cotton Bowl Athletic Association.

Gary Long wrote lessons four and five in this *Study Guide* and also "Teaching Plans" for lessons four and five in the *Adult Bible Teaching Guide*. Gary serves First Baptist Church, Gaithersburg, Maryland, as pastor, and formerly served Willow Meadows Baptist Church, Houston, Texas. He has also served churches in North Carolina and Virginia.

Randel Everett is executive director, Baptist General Convention of Texas. Dr. Everett wrote lessons six and seven. He formerly served churches in Texas, Arkansas, and Virginia and also served as founding president of the

John Leland Center for Theological Studies, Arlington, Virginia. He earned master's and doctoral degrees from Southwestern Baptist Theological Seminary.

William D. Shiell, writer of lessons eight through eleven, is senior pastor of First Baptist Church, Knoxville, Tennessee. He and his wife Kelly have two sons, Parker and Drake. He is the author of two books: *Reading Acts* (Brill, 2004) and *Sessions with Matthew* (Smyth and Helwys, 2008). He holds two degrees from Baylor University (Ph.D., New Testament; M.Div.) and one from Samford University (B.A.).

The Gospel of John: Light Overcoming Darkness, Part Two, The Light Overcomes

DATE OF STUDY

UNIT ONE

Jesus' Parting Message

UNIT TWO

Jesus' Trial and Crucifixion

UNIT THREE

Jesus' Resurrection

Introducing

THE GOSPEL OF JOHN:
Light Overcoming Darkness

The Gospel of John is many Christians' favorite book of the Bible. It contains wonderful and seemingly simple stories. Familiar incidents and passages in John 13—21 include these:

- Jesus washing the disciples' feet (John 13)
- Jesus' statement that he was *going to prepare a place for his disciples* (John 14)
- Jesus' prayer for his disciples (John 17)
- Jesus' appearance to Thomas (John 20)
- Jesus' questioning Peter about whether Peter truly loved him (John 21)

A Closer Look

One way of reading and studying the Gospel of John is simply to think of and consider it in light of familiar passages like these, passages we may well have known for years. For all the seeming simplicity, though, a closer look at the Gospel of John reveals that it can and should be studied on a deeper level. For one thing, much of the first seventeen chapters of the Gospel of John is unique to it, not appearing in the Gospels of Matthew, Mark, or Luke. Look back at the list in the previous section of familiar incidents and passages in John 13—21. None of those incidents and teachings appear in the other Gospels. They are unique to the Gospel of John.

Of course, we see some familiar incidents in John's Gospel that also appear in one or more of the other Gospels—Jesus feeding the 5,000, for example (John 6)—but even this incident is handled differently and interpreted in much greater depth and detail than in the other Gospels. Only when we get to Jesus' arrest (John 18:1–11), trial (John 18:12—19:15), crucifixion (John 19:16–42), and resurrection (John 20) do we find ourselves moving in territory that seems familiar because of our study of the other Gospels. Even here, though, comparing the Gospel of John to the other Gospels shows John's special approach.

The Gospel of John is structured uniquely, too. Many New Testament students have observed that the Gospel of John splits fairly neatly into two major parts. John 1—12 is often referred to as *the Book of Signs*. The second major part of the Gospel is John 13—21. In this portion, John 13—20 is referred to as *the Book of Glory*, with John 21 as an epilogue.

The Theme of the Gospel of John

One way to state the theme of the Gospel of John is to combine the thoughts of John 1:5, "The light shines in the darkness, and the darkness did not overcome it," and 1:11, "He came to what was his own, and his own people did not accept him." So the title of the first part of the Gospel, John 1—12, could be stated as *The Light Shines,* and the title of the second part, John 13—21, as *The Light Overcomes.* The Gospel of John is thus the story of *Light Overcoming Darkness.* This study of John 13—21 reminds us that truly *The Light Overcomes.*

A Previous Study: Part One of the Gospel of John (John 1—12)

A study of the first major part of the Gospel of John is provided in a previous volume—*The Gospel of John: Light Overcoming Darkness, Part One, The Light Shines (John 1—12)* (Dallas, Texas: BaptistWay Press, 2010).[1]

After a lesson on the prologue in John 1:1–18, *The Gospel of John: Light Overcoming Darkness, Part One, The Light Shines (John 1—12)* focuses on the signs by which Jesus revealed his identity in John 2—11. That study also emphasizes how Jesus, God's Son, signified his identity by superseding various Jewish rituals and institutions—purification practices (John 2); the temple (John 2); the learning of the rabbis (John 3); and all sacred places (John 4). *The Gospel of John: Light Overcoming Darkness, Part One, The Light Shines (John 1—12)* also considers how Jesus taught who he was by using the vehicles of Jewish festivals—the Sabbath (John 5); Passover (John 2:13–25; 6:1–71; see also 12—20); Booths (Tabernacles, John 7—9); and Dedication (*Hanukkah*, John 10:22–39).

This Study: Part Two of the Gospel of John (John 13—21)

The second major part of the Gospel of John, chapters 13—21, deals with Jesus in the last week of his earthly life and then in a week and an additional short amount of time beyond. John 13—17 focuses on Jesus and the disciples in the upper room. In these chapters, Jesus gave parting words of instruction, challenge, and encouragement to his disciples. These chapters contain Jesus' example of servanthood in washing the disciples' feet (John 13); his assertion that he himself was "the way, and the truth, and the life" (14:6); his teachings about the Holy Spirit (John 14—16); his challenge to the disciples to "go and bear fruit" (15:16); and his prayer that his disciples be united in him (John 17).

Chapters 18—19 continue with the events and meaning of Jesus' trial and crucifixion. Then chapters 20—21 deal with four resurrection appearances of Jesus.

As We Continue to Study

A brilliant Baptist interpreter of the Gospel of John, George Beasley-Murray,[2] taught the New Testament in both the United States and Great Britain and is now gone to be with the Lord of whom this Gospel is written. He suggested that the Gospel of John can speak to people in various life situations. New believers can find in John a wonderful exposition of the faith they have embraced. Mature Christians can continue to find their faith illumined as they learn more of Jesus through this Gospel. Aged Christians can learn even more of the glory of God as it is revealed in this Gospel. Those who are dying can find comfort in its words that tell of Jesus' bringing peace, comfort, and hope.

Let us add that those who have not yet believed can be led to believe through a study of this Gospel. As the Gospel of John states, "Jesus did many other signs in the presence of his disciples, which are not written in this book. But these are written so that you may come to believe that Jesus is the Messiah, the Son of God, and that through believing you may have life in his name" (20:30–31).

Which vantage point is yours? Whatever the case, as you continue to study this Gospel, let John's message speak to you.

UNIT ONE. JESUS' PARTING MESSAGE

Lesson 1	Jesus' New Approach to Human Relationships	John 13:1–17
Lesson 2	Jesus—Truly the Way	John 13:31—14:14
Lesson 3	The Spirit—Continuing Jesus' Ministry	John 14:15–18, 25–27; 15:26—16:15
Lesson 4	Demanded of Disciples	John 15:1–17
Lesson 5	Jesus' Prayer for His Disciples—Including You	John 17

UNIT TWO. JESUS' TRIAL AND CRUCIFIXION

Lesson 6	Judging Jesus	John 18:15–27; 18:33—19:16
Lesson 7	Dying to Bring Life	John 19:16b–30, 38–42

UNIT THREE. JESUS' RESURRECTION

Lesson 8	Good News About Jesus	John 20:1–18
Lesson 9	Sent to Continue Jesus' Ministry	John 20:19–23
Lesson 10	Confessing Who Jesus Is	John 20:24–31
Lesson 11	Follow Jesus—No Excuses	John 21:1–23

Additional Resources for Studying the Gospel of John[3]

George R. Beasley-Murray. *John*. Word Biblical Commentary. Volume 36. Second edition. Waco, Texas: Word Books, Publisher, 1999.

Raymond E. Brown. *The Gospel According to John (I—XII)*. Garden City, New York: Doubleday & Company, Inc., 1966.

Raymond E. Brown. *The Gospel According to John (XIII—XXI)*. Garden City, New York: Doubleday & Company, Inc., 1970.

F.F. Bruce. *The Gospel of John.* Grand Rapids, Michigan: William B. Eerdmans Publishing Company, 1983.

Gary M. Burge, *The* NIV *Application Commentary: John.* Grand Rapids, Michigan: Zondervan Publishing House, 2000.

James E. Carter. *John.* Layman's Bible Book Commentary. Volume 18. Nashville: Broadman Press, 1984.

Herschel H. Hobbs. *The Gospel of John: Invitation to Life.* Nashville, Tennessee: Convention Press, 1988.

William E. Hull. "John." *The Broadman Bible Commentary.* Volume 9. Nashville, Tennessee: Broadman Press, 1970.

Craig S. Keener. *The Gospel of John: A Commentary.* Two volumes. Peabody, Massachusetts: Hendrickson Publishers, 2003.

Lesslie Newbigin. *The Light Has Come: An Exposition of the Fourth Gospel.* Grand Rapids, Michigan: William B. Eerdmans Publishing Company, 1982.

Gail R. O'Day. "The Gospel of John." *The New Interpreter's Bible.* Volume IX. Nashville, Tennessee: Abingdon Press, 1995.

NOTES ————————————————————————————

1. See www.baptistwaypress.org, or call 1–866–249–1799.

2. George R. Beasley-Murray, *John*, Word Biblical Commentary, vol. 36 (Waco, Texas: Word Books, Publisher, 1987), x.

3. Listing a book does not imply full agreement by the writers or BAPTISTWAY PRESS® with all of its comments.

——— U N I T O N E ———
Jesus' Parting Message

The focus of this first unit in Part Two of *The Gospel of John: Light Overcoming Darkness* is on John 13—17. The five lessons deal with Jesus' instructions to and encouragement of the disciples in the upper room on the night before his crucifixion. These chapters contain Jesus' example of servanthood in washing the disciples' feet (John 13); his assertion that he himself is "the way, and the truth, and the life" (14:6); his teachings about the Holy Spirit (John 14—16); his challenge to the disciples to "go and bear fruit" (15:16); and his prayer that his disciples be united (John 17).[1]

Lesson 5 Jesus' Prayer for His Disciples—   John 17
              Including You

NOTES

1. Unless otherwise indicated, all Scripture quotations in lessons
   one through three are from the New International Version and
   all quotations in lessons four and five are from the New Revised
   Standard Version.

LESSON ONE

Jesus' New Approach to Human Relationships

MAIN IDEA

Jesus' example to the disciples turns human ideas of status and service upside down (or right side up) and challenges his followers to follow his example in their relationships with others.

QUESTION TO EXPLORE

In what ways do you act as a servant as Jesus did?

STUDY AIM

To summarize the meaning of Jesus' example to his disciples and to identify ways I will follow Jesus' example of service in my relationships with others.

QUICK READ

Jesus surprised and perplexed his disciples by taking on the role of the servant to wash their feet. In doing so, Jesus reminded his disciples that he had set an example to be followed in their relationships with others.

A member of a local church made a visit to his pastor to let the pastor know that he and his family would be moving their membership to another church. When the pastor inquired why they would be moving their membership, the man replied that they weren't being fed at this church. The pastor responded by telling the man that maybe he should take off the bib and put on the towel.

When Jesus put on the towel, he was turning self-centeredness and status on its head. He was instructing his disciples that they should do for others as he had done for them.

Jesus used these final hours before his crucifixion to instruct and encourage his disciples (John 13—17). He reminded them that they were to follow his example of service. He encouraged them to not be afraid of his departure but to continue to obey his commands. He told them that although he would go away for a short period of time, he would come back to get them. He reminded them that they would be known as his disciples by the love they demonstrated for each other. He warned them to stay connected to him so they would bear fruit. He promised them the comfort and guidance of the Holy Spirit. He prayed for the unity and safety of his followers.

JOHN 13:1–17

¹ It was just before the Passover Feast. Jesus knew that the time had come for him to leave this world and go to

the Father. Having loved his own who were in the world, he now showed them the full extent of his love.

2 The evening meal was being served, and the devil had already prompted Judas Iscariot, son of Simon, to betray Jesus. **3** Jesus knew that the Father had put all things under his power, and that he had come from God and was returning to God; **4** so he got up from the meal, took off his outer clothing, and wrapped a towel around his waist. **5** After that, he poured water into a basin and began to wash his disciples' feet, drying them with the towel that was wrapped around him.

6 He came to Simon Peter, who said to him, "Lord, are you going to wash my feet?"

7 Jesus replied, "You do not realize now what I am doing, but later you will understand."

8 "No," said Peter, "you shall never wash my feet."

Jesus answered, "Unless I wash you, you have no part with me."

9 "Then, Lord," Simon Peter replied, "not just my feet but my hands and my head as well!"

10 Jesus answered, "A person who has had a bath needs only to wash his feet; his whole body is clean. And you are clean, though not every one of you." **11** For he knew who was going to betray him, and that was why he said not every one was clean.

12 When he had finished washing their feet, he put on his clothes and returned to his place. "Do you understand what I have done for you?" he asked them. **13** "You call me

'Teacher' and 'Lord,' and rightly so, for that is what I am.
14 Now that I, your Lord and Teacher, have washed your feet,
you also should wash one another's feet. **15** I have set you an
example that you should do as I have done for you. **16** I tell
you the truth, no servant is greater than his master, nor is a
messenger greater than the one who sent him. **17** Now that
you know these things, you will be blessed if you do them.

Doing What Is Customary (13:1–5)

The custom of Jesus' day was for the homeowner to provide a servant to wash the feet of his guests who had been
walking along dusty roads in sandals. When guests ate a
meal, they reclined at a low table, with each person's feet
very close to the other's face.

The Twelve walked up the stairs to the upper room.
The first disciple walked in the door, looked for the foot-
washing servant, and noticed he was not there. Should
the disciple wash his own feet? Should he take off his garment, become a servant, and wash everyone else's feet?
Each one came in, took his place at the table, and placed
dirty feet in the face of the one next to him.

Jesus came in, looked at the dirty feet of the disciples,
looked at the water, got up from the table, took off his
outer garment, wrapped a towel around his waist, and
proceeded to wash the disciples' feet. He demonstrated for
them servant leadership and showed them the full extent
of his love.

We live in a world where levels of importance are established by custom. We know who is important and who is not. Status resides in those who are successful in their chosen field. Someone with high status may be a politician, an actor, a sports figure, a religious personality, or a business tycoon. It is customary to defer to those of elevated status.

Jesus turns what is customary on its head. Jesus knew that he had come from the Father and would be returning to the Father. Jesus' nearness to God brought him closer to people instead of drawing him away from them. This is a telling spiritual characteristic. The closer we are to God, the closer we should be to others. John would make this point also in 1 John 4:12, "No one has ever seen God; but if we love one another, God lives in us and his love is made complete in us."

Jesus was well aware that the one who would betray him and the one who would deny him were in the group whose feet he would wash. Yet, instead of becoming bitter or resentful toward these men, Jesus displayed his humility and love. It is so easy and somewhat customary to resent those who deliberately try to hurt us. But Jesus turned this customary response upside down.

Doing What Is Exemplary (13:6–15)

After Jesus washed his disciples' feet, he said something to them that he said only once in the New Testament, "I have set you an example that you should do as I have done for you" (John 13:15). What prompted Jesus to set this kind of example?

The Gospel of Luke may shed a little more light on Jesus' motive as it gives more background to this meal in Luke 22:24. Luke wrote that as Jesus was approaching the most important moment in his life, his disciples were continuing to argue about who would be the greatest in the kingdom. Jesus was facing the ultimate sacrifice for salvation, and his disciples were arguing over petty things. This argument may have been what prompted Jesus to put on the towel and wash their feet.

Christians are still susceptible to arguing over petty things and ignoring the most important things. In too many congregations the desire for recognition and status creates unnecessary conflict. Many fights in the local church are not over theology but over power and politics. Instead of church members seeking to serve one another in love, they are seeking to control one another and have others serve them. Jesus turns this struggle on its head.

Jesus told his disciples explicitly that he was setting them an example that they should follow. Does this mean that Christians should regularly wash each other's feet as part of their worship? Although foot washing was a regular practice among early Baptists, it had gradually declined by the early 1800s. Some Baptist groups continue to practice foot washing in their worship services.

What does it mean to set an example? A young boy was watching his dad use a baseball bat to break ice off their driveway. When the father went into the house to get something warm to drink, the son stayed outside. In a few minutes the son came into the house to proudly announce that he had broken the ice off the family car. When the dad asked him how he did it, the little boy replied, "The same way you did the driveway—with the baseball bat."

What did Jesus mean when he told his disciples he was setting them an example to follow? The word used for "example" in John 13:15 in the Greek New Testament could be translated *example, pattern, or illustration*. It is the spirit and not the action itself that is to be imitated. Jesus was not interested in instituting a new religious ceremony of foot washing but in setting an example of love, compassion, and service. Jesus washed the feet of the one who would betray him and the one who would deny him. His example demonstrated clearly what the Apostle Paul wrote later in Romans 5:8, "But God demonstrates his own love for us in this: While we were still sinners, Christ died for us."

Serving and sacrifice are at the heart of the Christian faith. In fact, Jesus made it very clear that one who did not deny himself could not be a disciple (Luke 9:23).

Doing What Is Necessary (13:16–17)

Many times we face the decision of doing what is convenient or doing what is necessary.

Many believers coast through life doing only that which is convenient. Jesus stresses that being a disciple demands doing what is necessary, humbly serving others.

Jesus emphasizes the importance of serving one another by saying, "I tell you the truth . . ." (John 13:16). The emphasis on "the truth" in the Greek New Testament is stressed by the double use of the Greek word *amen* at the beginning of the sentence. These two words are placed at the beginning of the sentence for emphasis. The words signify that this is a truth that is important and necessary for authentic discipleship. What is this truth? The truth is that "no servant is greater than his master" (13:16). If Jesus is truly the master of our life, we must be willing to serve as Jesus served. If we are going to be messengers of God's grace in Jesus Christ, we must serve like the One who sends the messenger. Jesus did not give his disciples this example for them to admire but for them to practice.

Maturity in Christ comes as one moves from selfishness to service. Maturity in Christ comes as one moves from the world's value system to Christ's value system. Jesus knew the weakness of human flesh. He knew his disciples would battle what humans generally have to battle— the feeling that they are as good as if not superior to certain others. With his example, Jesus gives his disciples another comparison to make. They are no longer to compare themselves to other people but to Jesus. If any believer considers himself or herself too important to stoop to serve someone else, then that person has come to consider himself or herself greater than Jesus.

Years ago an older and wiser pastor pointed to a cocky and self-assured young pastor and said, "There, but for the grace of God, goes God himself." Jesus taught that a *great person* was one who set an example by serving others (Matthew 20:26).

Simon Peter protested what Jesus was doing for him. Jesus assured Peter that although he did not understand now, he would understand later. It would be a hard lesson for Peter to learn, but he would later render a similar service of humility. Jesus' example made a lasting impression on Peter (1 Peter 5:5).

Jesus promises a blessing to those who humbly serve others. When we serve as Jesus served, we are truly "blessed" (John 17:17). Being "blessed" means that disciples of Jesus will have the joy of Jesus as they serve. Being "blessed" means disciples of Jesus will have a sense of wholeness within themselves as they serve. The *blessing* is a promise of Jesus. The *blessing* comes not from simply *knowing* but from *doing*. The action of the Greek verb translated "do" means *to keep on doing* on every occasion (17:17). Disciples of Jesus will not be diminished in any way through humble service to others.

A recent study indicates that we feel good when we are nice to others. In the study, a group of people were each given $128 of real money. They could choose to keep the money or to give it to a charity of their choice. The study revealed that when people chose to give the money, their brains experienced positive feelings, sometimes more intense than having been given the money in the first place.[1]

Jesus turns human ideas of status and service upside down. Instead of receiving a greater blessing by getting, we receive a greater blessing by giving. Giving is a necessity for the disciple of Jesus Christ.

For Life Today

John's account of Jesus washing his disciples' feet reminds us of some important truths concerning discipleship. In the first place, Jesus' example turned the idea of status upside down. Even though Jesus was their Lord and teacher, he took on the role of their servant.

Discipleship requires service to others.

Second, Jesus not only served those who loved him but also those who would betray him and deny him. Discipleship requires serving others who may not agree with us or may not like us. Discipleship requires that as messengers of Jesus Christ we carry the same message of loving service to our world that he carried.

Finally, discipleship requires more than knowledge. It requires doing. The blessing of God comes from the doing of service for others.

THE DEVIL AND JUDAS

John 13:2 states that "the devil had already prompted Judas Iscariot, son of Simon, to betray Jesus." (John 13:2). The Greek New Testament reads literally, *the devil already having placed (or put) into the heart.*

What does it mean *to put or place something into the heart or to prompt someone to do something*? Putting or placing an idea into someone's heart or mind is done through the power of suggestion. A suggestion that is attractive or tempting to someone is offered as a possibility.

How and why would the devil be successful in putting betrayal into Judas's heart? The perfect tense of the verb for *put* or *place* indicates that Judas had the thought for some time and had let it simmer until he finally acted. It may be that Satan used the decree of the Sanhedrin in John 11:57. That decree might have sounded attractive to Judas. Or, it could have been that Satan entered Judas's heart through greed (John 12:4–6). In fact, Matthew 26:14–16 indicates this. Greed very possibly could have become an appealing temptation to Judas.

We are reminded that it isn't just Judas that Satan seeks to influence and destroy. It is each one of us. We are to resist him in the faith (1 Peter 5:8–9).

CASE STUDY

The CEO of your company has been very difficult as an employer. He doesn't seem to care for you and has passed you over for several promotions. Working for him has made your life difficult.

You learn that this CEO is facing serious surgery that will require blood transfusions. You also learn that his blood type is very rare. You and some of your fellow employees know that you have that rare blood type. Do you offer to give blood for this CEO, or do you wait, hoping someone else will give?

QUESTIONS

1. How do you think Jesus knew his time had come to leave this world?

2. Why did Simon Peter not want Jesus to wash his feet?

3. What type of people do you find difficulty serving?

4. On what occasions have you washed someone's feet?

NOTES

1. Jonah Lehrer, *How We Decide* (Boston-New York: Houghton Mifflin Harcourt, 2009), 184)

LESSON TWO

Jesus—
Truly the Way

MAIN IDEA

Jesus' provision of himself as the way to the Father's presence encourages disciples to trust and serve him.

QUESTION TO EXPLORE

How does Jesus' provision of himself as the way to the Father affect your life?

STUDY AIM

To summarize the meaning of Jesus' conversation with Peter, Thomas, and Philip and to describe how it offers encouragement to disciples today

QUICK READ

Jesus used the occasion of his approaching death to reassure the disciples of God's continuing presence with them. In seeing Jesus, Thomas and Philip were seeing God. In knowing Jesus, one could know God. In trusting Jesus, one is trusting God.

Several years ago my wife and I visited North Carolina as part of a genealogical study trip. We stopped at a paint store in the small town of Dallas, North Carolina, to ask for directions to the local library. The proprietor of the paint store asked why we wanted to go the library. I explained that we were doing genealogical research on my ancestors from North Carolina. He said, "Oh, you don't need to go to the library. You need the retired postmaster. He knows everything about this area. I will call him for you." He called the postmaster and made arrangements for my wife and me to be guided around the area. Instead of being told where to find gravesites of early ancestors, the postmaster accompanied us and showed us what we wanted to know.

Jesus not only told his disciples that he was the way, the truth, and the life, but he also told them that he would go and prepare a place for them and come back to get them (John 14:6). He told them these things to encourage them to trust and serve him.

The ultimate question for every human being is this: *What will happen to me when I die?* In his conversations with Peter, Thomas, and Philip, Jesus answered the where and how of life and death. The Jesus present with these disciples in life would be the same Jesus present with them in death. The trust these disciples placed in Jesus in life would carry them to the place Jesus had prepared for them. Jesus was the way to the Father, the truth about the

Father, and the life in the Father. The presence of God in Jesus would encourage these disciples to trade a troubled heart for a trusting heart.

JOHN 13:31–38

31 When he was gone, Jesus said, "Now is the Son of Man glorified and God is glorified in him. **32** If God is glorified in him, God will glorify the Son in himself, and will glorify him at once.

33 "My children, I will be with you only a little longer. You will look for me, and just as I told the Jews, so I tell you now: Where I am going, you cannot come.

34 "A new command I give you: Love one another. As I have loved you, so you must love one another. **35** By this all men will know that you are my disciples, if you love one another."

36 Simon Peter asked him, "Lord, where are you going?"

Jesus replied, "Where I am going, you cannot follow now, but you will follow later."

37 Peter asked, "Lord, why can't I follow you now? I will lay down my life for you."

38 Then Jesus answered, "Will you really lay down your life for me? I tell you the truth, before the rooster crows, you will disown me three times!

JOHN 14:1–14

1 "Do not let your hearts be troubled. Trust in God; trust also in me. **2** In my Father's house are many rooms; if it were not so, I would have told you. I am going there to prepare a place for you. **3** And if I go and prepare a place for you, I will come back and take you to be with me that you also may be where I am. **4** You know the way to the place where I am going."

5 Thomas said to him, "Lord, we don't know where you are going, so how can we know the way?"

6 Jesus answered, "I am the way and the truth and the life. No one comes to the Father except through me. **7** If you really knew me, you would know my Father as well. From now on, you do know him and have seen him."

8 Philip said, "Lord, show us the Father and that will be enough for us."

9 Jesus answered: "Don't you know me, Philip, even after I have been among you such a long time? Anyone who has seen me has seen the Father. How can you say, 'Show us the Father'? **10** Don't you believe that I am in the Father, and that the Father is in me? The words I say to you are not just my own. Rather, it is the Father, living in me, who is doing his work. **11** Believe me when I say that I am in the Father and the Father is in me; or at least believe on the evidence of the miracles themselves. **12** I tell you the truth, anyone who has faith in me will do what I have been doing. He will do even greater things than these, because I am going to the Father. **13** And I will do whatever you ask in my name, so that the Son may bring glory to the Father. **14** You may ask me for anything in my name, and I will do it."

A Loving Presence (13:31–35)

As Jesus was preparing his disciples for his departure from the earth, he reminded them that although they would no longer have his physical presence they would still have one another. His presence would be experienced in part through their love for one another. It was to be a love modeled after his love for them. "As I have loved you" carries with it the idea of sacrificial love (John 13:34). God's supreme presence in the world came in the person of Jesus Christ. Further, God's supreme act in the world was an act of love—sacrificing his Son for the sins of humankind. John reminds us in his First Epistle that love comes from God and "Everyone who loves has been born of God and knows God" (1 John 4:7). John also reminds us that following the example of Jesus we should "lay down our lives for our brothers" (1 John 3:16). God's presence is made known in our lives through our sacrificial love for our brothers and sisters in Christ.

Jesus calls this a "new command," even though a similar command appears in the Old Testament, "love your

neighbor as yourself" (Leviticus 19:18). This commandment is "new" for at least three reasons: (1) It is new
because it is based on grace and not law. The disciples
were to love as Jesus loved—with grace. Grace means
gift. The disciples were to offer their love as a gift, not
as something earned or deserved. (2) It is new because it
narrows the focus from neighbor to "one another." It is
a love expressed among the believers in Jesus Christ and
based on a common relationship in Jesus Christ. (3) It
is new because it identifies an individual as a disciple of
Jesus Christ. A disciple is one who exercises discipline.
Loving one another is a Christian discipline. Loving
one another reveals the presence of Jesus in one's life.

As a seminary student I had the privilege of serving
on the staff of Dr. James Coggin at the Travis Avenue
Baptist Church in Fort Worth, Texas. Dr. Coggin was
a distinguished and wonderful leader. Several times
I heard him tell the story of how he was able to go to
college. Dr. Coggin came from humble circumstances.
When he graduated from high school, there was no
money for college. His sister, Willie, came to him and
gave him enough money to pay his first year's tuition.
When he asked where she got the money she told him
that she had sold her high school graduation ring. He
couldn't tell the story without tears in his eyes. What an
expression of loving sacrifice!

Jesus' presence is revealed in our lives through our love
for one another.

An Assuring Presence (13:36—14:5)

Peter was perplexed about where Jesus was going (John 13:36–38). Jesus reassured Peter that even though Peter could not follow immediately he would follow later. Peter would not only follow Jesus to heaven, but he also would follow Jesus by dying for the gospel (21:18–19). Following was defined by Jesus in John 14:1–5 as a place and a presence.

Jesus prefaced his revelation with an encouraging word and a call to trust him. Jesus encouraged the disciples to replace their troubled hearts with trusting hearts. They should stop being shaken and stirred up. Since they trusted in God, they should trust in him. The two words for "trust" are imperatives or commands (14:1). Jesus reminded them that he would not mislead them. He then listed four realities to trust.

The first reality Jesus promised his disciples was the assurance that there were many "rooms" in his Father's house. The "many" means that there is room to spare for all those who would trust in him. No one who trusts in Jesus Christ will be turned away from the Father's house for lack of space. God has a house, a home, to which believers will go. David wrote, "I will dwell in the house of the Lord forever" (Psalm 23:6). Everything that is comforting or attractive about a home is applied to heaven.

Second, Jesus promised them he was going "to prepare a place" for them. The Book of Hebrews says that Jesus "went before us" and "entered on our behalf" (Hebrews 6:20). Jesus went before us into heaven to prepare a place for us in God's house. When we prepare a place for Jesus in our hearts, he prepares a place for us in his home. The presence of Jesus makes the room ready for our reception.

Next, Jesus said he would come back to take them to be with him. There have been several interpretations of this promise. Some have seen this as a reference to the resurrection of Jesus. Others have applied it to the coming of the Holy Spirit (John 14:18). Still others say this statement refers to the death of the believer. Finally, there are those who believe this statement refers to the Second Coming of Jesus. Since Jesus says that when he comes he will take the disciples to be with him, it appears that this refers to the accompanying presence of Jesus in death. This understanding was brought home to me in the tragic death of one of our teenage church members. He and a friend were driving on a rural road when the vehicle overturned and killed the friend. I was called to the trauma room at 6:00 a.m. to be with the family of the dead teenager. The boy's father was very irate. He said to me, "Where was your God when my son died?" God gave me this immediate response, "God was where you and I couldn't be. God was going through death with your son."

Finally, Jesus promised they would be present with him. Whatever else heaven means, it means the presence of Jesus Christ. Being in heaven means being with Jesus, the One who loved us and died for us. It means seeing him clearly and knowing him fully (1 Corinthians 13:12).

A Saving Presence (14:6–10)

The doubts of Thomas led to one of Jesus' greatest truths. Jesus did not tell Thomas he would show him the way. Jesus told him *he* was "the way." Jesus did not tell Thomas he would show him the truth. Rather, Jesus told him *he* was "the truth." Jesus did not tell Thomas he would show him the life. Jesus told him *he* was "the life." There is a definite article in front of each description of Jesus: *the* way, *the* truth, *the* life. This way, truth, and life is found in a Person. Only by trusting in this Person, Jesus, can we be brought to God and dwell in God's house forever.

Jesus is the only way to the Father. Through Jesus' sacrificial death, he became the way to God. It was through his payment for sin that we have become reconciled (*made a friend*) to God.

Jesus is the embodiment of the truth of God. He is the reality of the grace of God coming into our lives. The law was given by Moses but grace and truth came through Jesus Christ (John 1:17).

Jesus is the life. He has become life for us. The Scriptures remind us that "the wages of sin is death, but the gift of God is eternal life in Christ Jesus our Lord" (Romans 6:23).

Philip did not fully comprehend what Jesus said to Thomas. He asked Jesus to show them the Father. Jesus responded by telling Philip that seeing Jesus is seeing the Father. Jesus was not speaking his own words but was speaking the words of the Father. Jesus was fully man and fully God. Paul reminds us that in Jesus dwelled "all the fullness of the Deity . . . in bodily form" (Colossians 2:9).

An Enabling Presence (14:11–14)

Jesus promised his disciples that they would do "greater things" than he had done (John 14:12). Does this mean greater in degree or greater in scope? Would followers of Jesus do anything greater than multiplying loaves and fishes, healing the sick, or raising the dead? What Jesus promised to his followers was the power of his enabling presence to go beyond the physical limits placed on him while he was on the earth. Jesus never went beyond Palestine with the gospel. His earthly sphere of influence was confined to a small geographical area. The ability of his followers to do greater things came from his return to his Father (14:12). Jesus promised that when he returned to the Father, the Holy Spirit would come (16:7). The enabling presence of the Holy Spirit allowed his followers to work in scattered places and influence larger numbers. When Jesus was in the flesh, he was limited by time and space, but when he went to the Father, he was liberated from the limitations of the flesh. His Holy Spirit was set free to operate throughout the world.

Physical miracles reveal the power and goodness of God, but spiritual miracles (the salvation of one's soul) reveal the full grace of God in Jesus Christ. The great things deal with that which is physical. The "greater things" deal with that which is spiritual (5:20–21). Physical miracles are limited in time to this life. Spiritual miracles are eternal.

As followers of Jesus Christ, we have the enabling presence of Jesus Christ to do the greater things (greater than the physical miracles). We have the enabling presence to share the gospel of Jesus Christ in the power of the Holy Spirit.

The first church I served as pastor was a small country church in the Ozark Mountains. A mother and her two sons and one daughter began attending the church. After attending for a period of time, the three children professed faith in Jesus Christ. I visited in the home to talk with them about baptism. The father was not a Christian and was rather hostile to the idea of their baptism. Finally, the father agreed to let the children be baptized. They were baptized in the War Eagle River with their father in attendance. After I had left the church to attend seminary, I received a phone call informing me that one of the boys had been killed in a hunting accident. The family requested that I return and conduct the memorial service. When I drove into the yard of that country mountain home, the first person to greet me was the dad. Tears filled his eyes as he began to thank me profusely for helping his son come to know Christ and for persisting in letting him be baptized. That was the *greater thing* Jesus was talking about.

For Life Today

There are many mysteries about life. There are many things we do not understand. Jesus helped shed light on some of those things. He reminded his disciples that true glorification comes from obedience and sacrifice.

Too, Jesus also reminded his disciples that the authentic mark of a disciple is love for fellow believers. Jesus gave a clear plan for being certain that we know God and we know the way to God.

Further, Jesus reassured every believer that there would be room for them in God's house. Then Jesus concluded this section by reminding believers that they would have the enabling power to do greater things than he did while on the earth. It is God's presence in Christ and in us that allows us to serve him daily.

THE GLORIFICATION OF JESUS

The glorification of Jesus appears to be the opposite of what we think of as glorification. It is a paradox. We ordinarily think of glorification as honor, recognition, status, and reward. We don't usually associate glorification with obedience and suffering. Jesus' glorification began with his crucifixion between two criminals. His glorification continued in his resurrection. His glorification proceeded to his heavenly home. His glorification culminated in his return to earth.

Every aspect of the glorification of Jesus demonstrated God's love for his creation. God loves the world so much that he gave his only Son to die for our sins. Every aspect of Jesus' life and ministry gave glory to God (John 2:11; 11:4; 17:4; 17:10).

Jesus was glorified not to bring honor to himself but to bring honor to God through his obedience. A child who obeys a parent brings honor to that parent.

Paul reminds us that because Jesus submitted himself to death on the cross, God highly exalted him (Philippians 2:6–11). Jesus brought honor to God through his obedience, and God brought honor to Jesus by elevating his name above all names.

MANY PATHS TO GOD?

Your company has relocated you to a multicultural community. You work with people from all over the world. They represent different lifestyles and different religious beliefs.

An employee about your age, with a young family like yours, befriends you. You play racquetball together and occasionally go out to dinner.

This friend believes there are many paths to God. He believes everyone will eventually go to heaven. How do you help him understand that Jesus is "the way and the truth and the life" and that "no one comes to the Father except through" Jesus (John 14:6)?

QUESTIONS

1. In what ways can we glorify God today?

2. How do we show Christ's love to our fellow believers?

3. What other ways do people try to get to heaven rather than through Jesus, who is "the way and the truth and the life"?

4. When has the Holy Spirit led you to share the gospel?

LESSON THREE

The Spirit— Continuing Jesus' Ministry

MAIN IDEA

The sending of the Spirit provides for the continuing ministry and presence of Jesus in and through his disciples.

QUESTION TO EXPLORE

How can we continue to live and minister on Jesus' behalf in a world like this?

STUDY AIM

To describe the ministry of the Spirit and to identify ways the Spirit's ministry provides me encouragement and strength for Christian living and ministry

QUICK READ

Jesus promised the internal and eternal presence of the Holy Spirit to every believer. The Holy Spirit would be just like Jesus, encouraging and guiding his followers.

While attending and speaking at a missionary conference in Interlaken, Switzerland, I was offered the opportunity to parasail over the Swiss Alps. The offer came from my wife in the form of a dare. She and I had watched people parasailing high over the Alps and finally landing in a grassy area in the town center. She urged me to join her in this adventure. After giving all the reasons I didn't think it was a good idea, I finally relented, concluding that I would rather die parasailing over the Alps than to listen for the rest of my life to my wife's accusations of cowardice.

As luck would have it, I was assigned to be the first off the mountain. The guide who would fly with me assured me that he would be with me the entire flight and would instruct me on everything I needed to do. He said, "Just listen to me, do what I tell you, and you will have a great and successful experience." He was right!

As Jesus was preparing his disciples for his departure from the earth, he assured them that he would not leave them as "orphans" (John 15:18). He told them that God would send another one just like him to encourage and guide them even in the face of hatred and persecution. He promised that the Spirit would be in them to remind them of everything Jesus had taught them in order to assist them in their ministries. Jesus instructed them to obey all he commanded them so they would remain in his love and live spiritually fruitful lives. Jesus told his disciples the Spirit within them would strengthen their testimony in convincing the world of guilt, righteousness, and judgment. These final words from Jesus were given to provide encouragement and strength for Christian living and ministry.

JOHN 14:15–18, 25–27

15 "If you love me, you will obey what I command. **16** And I will ask the Father, and he will give you another Counselor to be with you forever— **17** the Spirit of truth. The world cannot accept him, because it neither sees him nor knows him. But you know him, for he lives with you and will be in you. **18** I will not leave you as orphans; I will come to you.

• • • • • • • • • • • • • • • • • • • •

25 "All this I have spoken while still with you. **26** But the Counselor, the Holy Spirit, whom the Father will send in my name, will teach you all things and will remind you of everything I have said to you. **27** Peace I leave with you; my peace I give you. I do not give to you as the world gives. Do not let your hearts be troubled and do not be afraid.

JOHN 15:26–27

26 "When the Counselor comes, whom I will send to you from the Father, the Spirit of truth who goes out from the Father, he will testify about me. ²⁷ And you also must testify, for you have been with me from the beginning.

JOHN 16:1–15

¹ "All this I have told you so that you will not go astray. ² They will put you out of the synagogue; in fact, a time is coming when anyone who kills you will think he is offering a service to God. ³ They will do such things because they have not known the Father or me. ⁴ I have told you this, so that when the time comes you will remember that I warned you. I did not tell you this at first because I was with you.

⁵ "Now I am going to him who sent me, yet none of you asks me, 'Where are you going?' ⁶ Because I have said these things, you are filled with grief. ⁷ But I tell you the truth: It is for your good that I am going away. Unless I go away, the Counselor will not come to you; but if I go, I will send him to you. ⁸ When he comes, he will convict the world of guilt in regard to sin and righteousness and judgment: ⁹ in regard to sin, because men do not believe in me; ¹⁰ in regard to righteousness, because I am going to the Father, where you can see me no longer; ¹¹ and in regard to judgment, because the prince of this world now stands condemned.

¹² "I have much more to say to you, more than you can now bear. ¹³ But when he, the Spirit of truth, comes, he will guide you into all truth. He will not speak on his own; he will speak only what he hears, and he will tell you what is yet to

come. **14** He will bring glory to me by taking from what is mine and making it known to you. **15** All that belongs to the Father is mine. That is why I said the Spirit will take from what is mine and make it known to you.

An Encouraging Presence (14:15–18)

Jesus promised his disciples he would "give" them another Counselor (14:16). The word translated "Counselor" is the Greek word *parakletos*. This is a compound Greek word made up of two words: *para*, meaning *along-side*, and *kaleo*, meaning *to call*. The disciples did not work for the presence of the Holy Spirit. He was a *gift* from God through a request of Jesus. It was God who sent the Spirit, not the disciples who earned the Spirit. He was a gift not an achievement.

Jesus referred to this gift of God as "another Counselor." The Greek word for "another" is *allos*—meaning *another of the same kind*. This Counselor would be One just like Jesus. Jesus would not leave his followers as "orphans" but would come to them as "another" just like him. This "Counselor" would minister through believers just as Jesus did: preaching, teaching, healing, and proclaiming the grace of God.

The word for "Counselor" indicates that this One is *called alongside* a believer for several purposes. He is called alongside to *encourage* believers. Encouraging believers involves a number of things: coming alongside another as an advocate in a court of law to offer a defense; coming alongside another in times of trial or crisis to bring comfort; and coming alongside another to help or strengthen in time of need.

Best-selling author Bruce Feiler was diagnosed with a bone tumor at forty-three years of age. He sat on a curb and cried after he had received the diagnosis. Then his mind turned to his twin three-year-old daughters who might grow up without him. He thought of all the things he would not get to do with them: teach them to ride a bike, go to school activities, watch them graduate, walk them down the aisle to get married, become a grandfather. As Feiler pondered his absence as a father, he came up with an idea: form a council of dads from friends who would embody some of his own characteristics. The title of his book is: *The Council of Dads: My Daughters, My Illness, and the Men Who Could Be Me.*[1]

As Jesus prepared to physically leave this earth, he promised his disciples that God would send someone just like him to minister with them, encourage them, defend them, comfort them, and strengthen them. Jesus could have entitled a book, *My Disciples, My Departure, and the One Who Could Be Me.*

Every believer is encouraged by Jesus to love him by obeying his commands so that they might experience this dynamic relationship with the Spirit. It is through love and obedience that a vital connection to the Spirit is maintained. In John 14:21, Jesus said he would "show myself to" the one who loves and obeys him. It is this encouraging presence that strengthens a believer in Christian living and ministry.

A Guiding Presence (14:25–27; 16:13–15)

Jesus not only promises an encouraging presence but also a guiding presence. The Holy Spirit will guide believers by teaching them "all things" and "reminding" them of "everything" Jesus said to them (14:26). In 16:13, Jesus referred to the Holy Spirit as "the Spirit of truth" who will "guide you into all truth." The Spirit and truth are intimately tied together.

The disciples of Jesus did not have a New Testament with the words of Jesus printed in red ink. They didn't have the ability to go to a concordance and look up things Jesus had taught. Therefore, it was the work of the Spirit to teach them and remind them. The Spirit speaks to believers what he hears from God (16:13) and points out the things of Jesus to them (16:14). Through the Spirit, Jesus becomes not a memory but a presence to be experienced by every believer—"the Spirit will take from what is mine and make it known to you" (16:15).

Believers today have God's word through Jesus in printed form. We have the opportunity to read, meditate on, and memorize the teachings of Jesus. As we read the words of Jesus, the Spirit guides us into "all truth." The Spirit guides us into a growing understanding or apprehension of God's truth. This is a part of the discipleship ministry of the Spirit. This is the work of sanctification, becoming holy. It is the work of maturing as a believer. The absolute and complete work of Jesus on earth becomes more intelligible through the continuing guidance of the Holy Spirit even as we become more mature in our understanding.

Theologians speak of our Scriptures as the *revelation of God* because they have been revealed to us. Theologians also speak of the *illumination* of the Scriptures, which means that the Holy Spirit guides us in our understanding of that which has been revealed. Some people tell of reading the same Scripture several times and getting a different application for their life. This is the guiding and illuminating presence of the Spirit.

I serve as a volunteer chaplain for Sugar Land Methodist Hospital. Volunteer chaplains serve the hours from 5:00 p.m. to 7:00 a.m., so the regular chaplains can go home and get a break from the constant pressure of their job.

In the early morning hours, I received a call from a nurse in the labor and delivery area of the hospital. The nurse asked me to come and minister to a young mother who had delivered a stillborn baby girl. These kinds of life experiences are impossible to understand and explain.

When I arrived at the young mother's room, I was met by a grandmother and an aunt who related that they expected a healthy child but something went wrong in the delivery and the baby died. Everyone in the room was understandably distraught. The grandmother asked if I would take the baby out of the crib and let the mother hold her one last time. I did what she asked and stood next to her as she cradled the baby and spoke softly to the baby.

The mother looked up at me and asked why this had to happen. I told her I didn't know why. Just at that moment, the Holy Spirit guided me to these two Scriptures: "See that you do not look down on one of these little ones. For I tell you that their angels in heaven always see the face of my Father in heaven" (Matthew 18:10); "Jesus said, 'Let the little children come to me, and do not hinder them, for the kingdom of heaven belongs to such as these'" (Matt. 19:14).

After I read these Scriptures, we had prayer. The mother looked up at me and said, "Would you write those Scriptures and give them to me." The Spirit guided me into God's truth for that mother so she could receive his comfort and help in her time of need.

The words of Jesus are true: The Spirit will guide us into all truth and remind us of everything Jesus said.

A Convincing Presence (15:26—16:15)

The Spirit is not only an encouraging and guiding presence. He is also a convincing presence. Jesus told his disciples that the Spirit of truth would testify about Jesus. One of the ways we know the Spirit is testifying is to check out his subject. If someone is glorifying the Spirit, we know it is not the Spirit who is testifying. But if someone is glorifying Jesus, we know that it is the Spirit who is testifying—"he will testify about me" (John 15:26).

Right after saying that the Spirit would testify about him, Jesus told his disciples that they "also must testify" (15:27). Jesus would reiterate this teaching in Acts 1:8, "But you will receive power when the Holy Spirit comes on you; and you will be my witnesses in Jerusalem, and in all Judea and Samaria, and to the ends of the earth." This is how God is building his kingdom on earth and beyond the earth, through faithful witnesses accompanied by the Holy Spirit.

Many times believers become unnecessarily frightened about witnessing about Jesus. They confuse witnessing to people with converting people. Some refuse to witness about Jesus for fear of having their witness or testimony rejected. It is to these that Jesus directs his words in John 16:7–11. The Advocate will be with the believer who is witnessing, and the Advocate will do the convincing. We are the second witness. The Holy Spirit has already been working in the life of the unbeliever. Our testimony becomes convincing because the Holy Spirit has already spoken to the heart of the unbeliever.

An example of this is found in Acts 8:26–40. There we are told about Philip's encounter with an Ethiopian eunuch, "an important official in charge of all the treasury of Candace, queen of the Ethiopians." Here we see the work of the Holy Spirit preparing the heart of the eunuch as he read Isaiah 53. Then the Spirit directed Philip to complete the witness, "The Spirit told Philip, 'Go to that chariot and stay near it.'" Not only did the Spirit instruct Philip to go to the chariot, but the Spirit also accompanied him. The Spirit's presence was so convincing that the eunuch immediately requested baptism.

Our commission as believers is to share the good news of Jesus Christ. The work of the Holy Spirit is to *convict* or to *convince* one of personal guilt, the possibility of righteousness, and the certainty of judgment. The word *convict* or *convince* is the Greek word *elegchei*, meaning to demonstrate the truth to a person so the person sees it as truth. The word *elegchei* could also be translated *expose*. The Holy Spirit presents the truth in such a clear way that an unbeliever cannot fail to see it or deny it. We present the gospel, and the Holy Spirit makes it clear to the unbeliever. The Holy Spirit will convince a person that not to believe in Jesus Christ is to sin.

After Peter had preached his sermon on Pentecost, the Holy Spirit convicted the people listening. They were "cut to the heart and said to Peter and the other apostles, 'Brothers, what shall we do?' Peter replied, 'Repent and be baptized, every one of you, in the name of Jesus Christ for the forgiveness of sins, and you will receive the Holy Spirit'" (Acts 2:37–38).

When I was pastor of Metropolitan Baptist Church in Wichita, Kansas, a member of a ladies' prayer group came to tell me they had been praying for the salvation of the husband of one of their friends. She informed me that the man owned and operated a bar and grill only six blocks from our downtown church.

One morning I walked over to the bar and grill to introduce myself to the man. When I entered the bar, I asked for the owner, Merle Bates. A big, burly guy behind the bar said, "I am Merle Bates."

I said, "I am Phil Lineberger, the pastor of Metropolitan Baptist, and I wanted to drop by and say hello." When the customers heard *pastor*, they all stopped what they were doing to take a look. Since Merle was busy with customers, I told him I would come back later to visit.

Several weeks later I returned to the bar. Merle was alone when I returned. I said to him, "Merle, have you settled the question of a personal relationship with Jesus Christ, or are you still in the process?"

Merle looked at me and said, "Pastor, the day before you came in here the first time I was down on my knees in the keg room asking God to get me out of here."

We both started crying as I shared the gospel with Merle. He accepted Jesus as his Savior, and I had the privilege of baptizing him. His salvation and baptism energized our church like nothing else. God showed me that the Holy Spirit had gone before me and had already been working with Merle Bates, convincing him of sin, righteousness, and judgment.

For Life Today

Jesus' teachings on the Holy Spirit remind us of several tremendous spiritual truths. We have access to the same dynamic presence the disciples knew when Jesus ministered alongside them. One just like Jesus is present in our world and in our lives to minister with us and through us. No matter what problem we face or what difficulty we encounter, the Holy Spirit is present with us to be our encourager, advocate, helper, comforter, and guide.

As we witness to our faith in Jesus in an unbelieving world, the Holy Spirit accompanies that witness to convince those hearing that this is the truth of God. We should never fear sharing the gospel of Jesus Christ because it is the work of the Spirit to make the gospel convincing.

NEVER

"I will not leave you as orphans; I will come to you" (John 14:18). The phrase translated "I will come" is the Greek word *erchomai*, a present, active, indicative verb that can be translated, *I am coming*. *I am coming* is a promise from

Jesus of a perpetual, continual, and uninterrupted coming. There will never be a time in the life of the believer when he or she is left without the presence of the Comforter. That believer may have times in life when he or she does not access the presence of the Spirit because of disobedience or an unloving spirit, but the Spirit will always be coming to him or her.

Jesus could not always be with his disciples because of physical limitations such as time and space. But the Spirit is not limited by time and space. He is able to be everywhere at all times with all God's people, providing encouragement, guidance, and influence.

CASE STUDY

You work with a colleague who has experienced a devastating loss in his life. His daughter, the mother of four young children, was killed in an automobile accident caused by a drunk driver. The driver who caused the accident was uninjured.

Your colleague has been a believer for more than thirty years, is active in his church, and volunteers with a homeless shelter once a month. He tells you he feels God has abandoned him and his family. In addition to your presence, what spiritual truth could you share that would help him be aware of God's comforting and helping presence?

QUESTIONS

1. Why would God send the Holy Spirit to guide us into truth since we have his truth revealed in Scripture?

2. In what event in your life have you been aware of the Holy Spirit guiding you?

3. In what situations does the Holy Spirit act as an Advocate, coming to our defense?

4. Have you experienced a witnessing opportunity when you recognized that the Holy Spirit had gone before you?

NOTES

1. Bruce Feiler, *The Council of Dads: My Daughters, My Illness, and the Men Who Could Be Me* (New York: William Morrow, 2010).

LESSON FOUR
Demanded of Disciples

MAIN IDEA

Jesus' disciples are to stay vitally attached to him, demonstrating that attachment through radical obedience to Jesus and far-reaching love for one another.

QUESTION TO EXPLORE

Is anything demanded of disciples, or is it just a matter of saying we believe?

STUDY AIM

To describe how abiding in Christ, obeying Christ, and loving one another are related, and to analyze how I am expressing these demands of discipleship in my life

QUICK READ

Jesus instructed his disciples to stay connected to him and show love to one another. How do we do that?

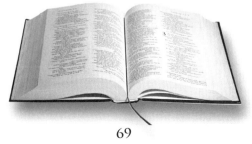

On my grandfather's North Carolina farm were two grapevines that seemed twenty feet tall in my child-sized memory but were only six or seven feet high in reality. The thick scuppernong vines draped heavily over a trellis of six ancient creosote posts. Tough hulls protected the fruit, and you had to squeeze the sweet innards in your mouth. They were pure sugar shots, especially good when the cool morning lingered in them. My cousin and I would hide beneath the vines to eat grapes in the shade, or we would fill our ball caps with grape bombs, climb high in the nearby magnolia tree, and see who could spit the hulls the furthest.

Sadly, only one of the vines remains. The other fell victim to bad pruning by someone who rented the place after my grandfather died nearly two decades ago. Perhaps the person who did the pruning thought the vine an eyesore and cut it all the way down to its main trunk. Or, maybe he pruned unknowingly into the current year's new growth. Whatever the reason, he didn't know how to prune a scuppernong vine carefully.

I've been thinking about that vine as I write this lesson on John 15. It's about Jesus the vine and us the branches. Jesus talked about grapevines to say that God is the vintner who prunes and shapes the vines to bear good fruit. Unlike that renter who pruned my grandfather's vines incorrectly, God prunes perfectly, shaping us to bear the good fruit of faithful living and fearless loving into a world that desperately needs the sweetness of the gospel.[1]

JOHN 15:1–17

1 "I am the true vine, and my Father is the vinegrower. **2** He removes every branch in me that bears no fruit. Every branch that bears fruit he prunes to make it bear more fruit. **3** You have already been cleansed by the word that I have spoken to you. **4** Abide in me as I abide in you. Just as the branch cannot bear fruit by itself unless it abides in the vine, neither can you unless you abide in me. **5** I am the vine, you are the branches. Those who abide in me and I in them bear much fruit, because apart from me you can do nothing. **6** Whoever does not abide in me is thrown away like a branch and withers; such branches are gathered, thrown into the fire, and burned. **7** If you abide in me, and my words abide in you, ask for whatever you wish, and it will be done for you. **8** My Father is glorified by this, that you bear much fruit and become my disciples. **9** As the Father has loved me, so I have loved you; abide in my love. **10** If you keep my commandments, you will abide in my love, just as I have kept my Father's commandments and abide in his love. **11** I have said these things to you so that my joy may be in you, and that your joy may be complete.

12 "This is my commandment, that you love one another as I have loved you. **13** No one has greater love than this, to lay down one's life for one's friends. **14** You are my friends if you do what I command you. **15** I do not call you servants any longer, because the servant does not know what the master is doing; but I have called you friends, because I have made known to you everything that I have heard from my Father. **16** You did not choose me but I chose you. And I appointed you to go and bear fruit, fruit that will last, so that the Father will give you whatever you ask him in my name. **17** I am giving you these commands so that you may love one another.

I Am the Vine (15:1–3)

"I am the true vine" is the last of the "I am" sayings from Jesus that John recorded.[2] Jesus has described himself as *the bread of life, the light of the world, the gate for the sheep, the good shepherd, the resurrection and the life,* and *the way, the truth, and the life.* This last "I am" statement also says the Father is the vinegrower. This statement is important for Bible students to note because it uses the agricultural images of grower, vine, and branches to expound on the interrelatedness of the Father, the Son, and the disciples.

Understanding ourselves as the branches is powerful imagery for understanding how we disciples are connected to the Father through the Son. First, there is the matter of nurture and growth. The proper nutrients for growth flow through the vine to the branches, and the proper nourishment we need as disciples flows to us through the teaching, ministry, life, death, and resurrection of Jesus. We are made strong by Jesus' connectedness to the Father.

But there is more. Remember my grandfather's scuppernong vine? I can still remember him pruning it carefully each season to enhance its fruit-bearing potential. Cut the vine back too harshly, and it may take years to recover. It might even die. Cut the vine back too little, and it will have lots of green leaves but very few grapes.

As the vinegrower, the Father removes all the branches that do not bear fruit. As the branches, we are already "cleansed" (John 15:3) by the word Jesus has given us. Note that this word has a double meaning of both pruning and cleansing in this context in the Greek. So there is this additional sense that the shaping and pruning of disciples come from the Father in order to create a meaningful tension of providing us resources for growth, as well boundaries and goals for growth.

Like my grandfather's careful pruning, God's pruning in our lives is neither too much nor too little. Rather, God works with us in relationship through the Son, Jesus, to mold us and shape us to bear fruit.

Christians are continually growing. No matter whether we've been Christians for seventy years or seventy days, we grow and are pruned. We have fruit to bear, but before we can bear much fruit we have to learn to abide in Jesus.

Abide in Me (15:4–7)

To the untrained eye, my grandfather's scuppernong vine looked like a big jumble of leaves, branches, and trunk. The creosote posts were not fancy, and the connecting beams of wood sagged with the history of the grapevine growth. But make no mistake about it, as messy as things may have appeared, each branch was connected to the vine, and the vine nourished each branch.

So it is in our discipleship. Notice the number of times the word "abide" occurs in the focal Scripture passage printed from the New Revised Standard Version in this *Study Guide*. (The word "remain" is used in the New International Version.) What does Jesus mean with the heavy use of this word "abide"?

Jesus envisioned a life for Christians that is intrinsically connected to him and, as we'll come to see in a moment, intrinsically connected to one another. *Abiding in Jesus* involves the development of a relationship between us and Jesus. *Abiding in Jesus* means spending time knowing and relating to the person of Jesus through Scripture, prayer, meditation, and everyday conversation with the resurrected Jesus, who is present and available to us. But Jesus also means something less mystical. *Abiding in Jesus* means keeping his commands, walking and talking as Jesus did, and thus acting out of kindness, love, justice, and mercy. *Abiding in Jesus* means that Jesus' way of doing things will be carried forward in the lives of his disciples.

Indeed, Jesus lives not only in the spiritual/mystical sense but also in the ways in which we conduct our lives.

Abiding in Jesus, then, is ultimately more than a metaphor about vines and branches. It is about a distinct kind of lifestyle. *Abiding in Jesus* is about living by a set of ethical demands that are framed by love and grace. Too, *abiding in Jesus* is about entering into that holy relationship as grateful recipients of God's goodness. You don't have to be a vintner to know that if the branches are cut off from the vine they will die. Yet, we often miss this and try to go at the spiritual journey all on our own. There is no such thing as an independent branch. Remember that vine of my grandfather's that looked like a jumbled mess? Not so. It was an interdependent and connected system, drawing nourishment from its one true vine, and bearing fruit into the world (and my stomach, hungry for a sweet grape!).

Bear Fruit (15:8–17)

The vineyard language did not sound foreign to the disciples who heard Jesus give his farewell discourse. Israel's history is filled with imagery from the vineyard. In Isaiah 5:7 we learn that ". . . the vineyard of the Lord of hosts is the house of Israel and the people of Judah are his pleasant planting. . . ." Isaiah 5:2 explains how God expected the vineyard to yield good grapes but instead it yielded sour grapes. You could document the entire history of Israel as a series of crop failures and successes, but God's ultimate success as a vintner came in the person of Jesus.

With Jesus as the true vine, God finally found a crop of grapes that would not turn sour. That's because God found in Jesus the supreme display of love, the ultimate fruit that God most deeply desires from the vineyard of our lives. Because Jesus became the life-giving fruit through his love, it is his love that we are instructed to duplicate.

"Abide in my love," Jesus said. This is the good fruit that we are to bear, and Jesus understands that bearing this love to the world will bring us complete joy (John 15:11). He becomes more specific beginning in verse 12. It is here that love becomes a command. This is not a pep talk, or a softly affirming motivational speech. Jesus moved to stronger language to say, essentially, *do* love.

Jesus defined the greatest love as the willingness to lay down one's life for one's friends. As Jesus gave this speech, that was precisely what he was about to do on behalf of the world. Anticipating his own death, he was describing to his disciples that love is ultimately about sacrifice for the benefit of others, a notion contrary and perhaps even offensive to our modern sensibilities that suggest that love is about our feelings or emotions toward another person. No, real love for one another has to be acted out, carried out, put into motion. Jesus did not likely *feel* very good or lovely about approaching the cross to die. But Jesus' action—laying down his life for his friends—showed his love in a non-negotiable way.

This passage also teaches us how Jesus views us: as "friends." We are not servants who are ignorant of what our master is doing, but rather we are close companions invited into intimacy and understanding of what Jesus is about. Until that moment in time, only Abraham bore the title "friend of God" (James 2:23), and yet we find the disciples, including us, given that very title as Jesus gave this love commandment.

Lest we grow too haughty, however, although we have been called "friends" (John 15:15), it is Jesus who has done the choosing (15:16). This emphasis is a stark reminder that the friend still has responsibility to obey Jesus in the same way a slave must obey a master. Being invited into intimacy with Jesus has the capacity to change our outward life toward our brothers and sisters. The unity this fosters helps us *branches* cling together and to the vine as we bear the fruit of love into the world.

No sour grapes there!

Implications and Actions

All this talk of vines, branches, and vinegrowers should get us thinking about how our lives bear fruit into the world. The implications are many, but here are a few ways of thinking about how this Bible passage can shape your life.

Life on the vine. The passage raises some basic questions about where you stand in your relationship to God. Are you connected fully to the vine, or do you sometimes feel you are just barely hanging on? Life on the vine calls for our attentiveness to things the world often neglects. In a world that values independence and self-reliance, this Bible passage calls us to rethink how we are truly dependent on God and on the community of God's people. If your life is a bit too chaotic, perhaps it's time to rely more on God, trusting in Jesus as your source of nurture and sustenance rather than being the *Lone Ranger.*

Abiding in Christ. Are you connected at some level to the vine, but do you feel the need for more nourishment? Are you a new Christian who wants to grow closer to Jesus? Perhaps it is a quiet call from God to strengthen your relationship with the living Jesus. He is alive and available to you, and many Christians have found the ancient practices of the church to be helpful in abiding in him (see the small article, "Spiritual Practices").

Bearing good fruit. Our lives must be fruitful, bearing the sweet fruit of love into the lives of others and in our interior worship to God. Bearing good fruit means we must also submit to the pruning of God. Where do you need pruning to bear better fruit? How can you produce sweetness in the lives of others? What things in your life are making your fruit bitter?

SPIRITUAL PRACTICES

How many times have you seen someone *crash and burn* in his or her life because the person didn't remain connected to Jesus? Has it happened to you? Some spiritual practices of the ancient church can help us stay connected to the True Vine:

- *Observing times of daily prayer.* Maintaining a regular set of times you will pray throughout the day will not only deepen your relationship with Jesus but also will help order your day in this overly busy life.

- *Keeping Sabbath.* Believers can benefit from the practice of limiting activities on the Sabbath to worship, rest, and family time.

- *Engaging in periods of silence and solitude.* Time alone helps us focus on God, and time in silence helps us tune out the noise of this world so we can hear the voice of God. Perhaps you could commit to spending two mornings per week in silence on the drive to work.

- *Fasting.* Abstaining from food for a period of time can sharpen our ability to listen to God and help us "abide" in Christ more closely.

PRODUCING FRUIT

The quality of a grape is affected by the soil, the weather, and the care the vine receives. Rich soil with the right balance of rain and sunshine are large parts of the equation, but the best grapes don't simply grow wild. They must be pruned and shaped during the dormant seasons in order to produce the sweetest, juiciest fruit in the growing season.

Pruning a grapevine calls for a juxtaposition of brutal cutting and tender precision. The best grapes grow off the wood that is one year old, and so the careful vintner has to know the vine well in order to get the best crop.

So it is with the Father (the Vinegrower). God knows us well and prunes us carefully, but prunes us nonetheless. Sometimes the pruning is painful, but it allows the possibility of new growth. This is not to say that all bad things in our lives are a result of God's pruning us, but our attitude should always be one that asks, *How can this difficulty produce better fruit in my life?*

QUESTIONS

1. Who is the vine? the grower? the branches?

2. How would you define the word "abide"?

3. "No one has greater love than this, to lay down one's life for one's friends" (John 15:13). For whom would you lay down your life? For whom should you be willing to lay down your life?

4. What events in your past do you understand now as God's pruning of your life?

5. Jesus calls us "friends" (John 15:15). How do you imagine this helps our light of faith overcome the darkness of the world?

6. *Making* fruit or *bearing* fruit? Is there a difference? If so, who does what? Where does God enter in? Where do we have responsibilities to bear or make fruit?

NOTES ————————————————————————

1. Unless otherwise indicated, all Scripture quotations in lessons four and five are from the New Revised Standard Version.

2. "I am the bread of life," John 6:35, 41, 48, 51; "I am the light of the world," 8:12; "I am the gate for the sheep," 10:7, 9; "I am the good shepherd," 10:11, 14; "I am the resurrection and the life," 11:25; "I am the way, and the truth, and the life," 14:6; "I am the true vine," 15:1, 5.

LESSON FIVE

Jesus' Prayer for His Disciples—Including You

MAIN IDEA

Jesus prayed for his disciples to be protected as they ministered on his behalf, and to be united with one another and in their relationship with himself and the Father.

QUESTION TO EXPLORE

Since Jesus prayed his followers would have unity in order to give credible witness to himself, why can't we at least get along better with one another?

STUDY AIM

To identify the main points of Jesus' prayer and to decide on ways I will implement them to get along better with fellow Christians

QUICK READ

Jesus' prayer in John 17 sets the stage for how, when, and what we should pray.

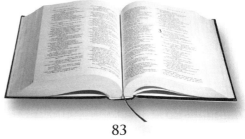

When something is said can increase the importance of the words themselves. That's the case with Jesus' words of prayer in John 17. This chapter contains Jesus' final prayer before he was led to the cross. It comes just after Jesus gave instruction to the disciples about what awaited him. Jesus uttered the prayer just before he was betrayed by Judas, handed over for a mockery of a trial, and then executed. Jesus was using his last moments to pray for himself, his disciples, and all believers to come. Even at the moment of his betrayal, faced with the hatred and bitterness of betrayal by Judas and those who sought to end his life, Jesus prayed on.

A prayer this important calls for a closer study. Let's look at the form and movements of Jesus' prayer, consider how much love filled him in those final moments, and how we might be transformed to love others in the same way. The prayer makes three basic moves. First, in verses 1–5, Jesus prayed for himself and his glory. Then in verses 6–19, Jesus prayed for his disciples. Finally, in verses 20–26, Jesus prayed for the ones who would come to believe because of the disciples' word—the church.

JOHN 17

1 After Jesus had spoken these words, he looked up to heaven and said, "Father, the hour has come; glorify your Son so that the Son may glorify you, **2** since you have given him authority over all people, to give eternal life to all whom you have given him. **3** And this is eternal life, that they may know you, the only true God, and Jesus Christ whom you have sent. **4** I glorified you on earth by finishing the work that you gave me to do. **5** So now, Father, glorify me in your own presence with the glory that I had in your presence before the world existed.

6 "I have made your name known to those whom you gave me from the world. They were yours, and you gave them to me, and they have kept your word. **7** Now they know that everything you have given me is from you; **8** for the words that you gave to me I have given to them, and they have received them and know in truth that I came from you; and they have believed that you sent me. **9** I am asking on their behalf; I am not asking on behalf of the world, but on behalf of those whom you gave me, because they are yours. **10** All mine are yours, and yours are mine; and I have been glorified in them. **11** And now I am no longer in the world, but they are in the world, and I am coming to you. Holy Father, protect them in your name that you have given me, so that they may be one, as we are one. **12** While I was with them, I protected them in your name that you have given me. I guarded them, and not one of them was lost except the one destined to be lost, so that the scripture might be fulfilled. **13** But now I am coming to you, and I speak these things in the world so that they may have my joy made complete in themselves. **14** I have given them your word, and the world has hated them because they do not

belong to the world, just as I do not belong to the world.
15 I am not asking you to take them out of the world, but I ask you to protect them from the evil one. **16** They do not belong to the world, just as I do not belong to the world.
17 Sanctify them in the truth; your word is truth. **18** As you have sent me into the world, so I have sent them into the world. **19** And for their sakes I sanctify myself, so that they also may be sanctified in truth.

20 "I ask not only on behalf of these, but also on behalf of those who will believe in me through their word, **21** that they may all be one. As you, Father, are in me and I am in you, may they also be in us, so that the world may believe that you have sent me. **22** The glory that you have given me I have given them, so that they may be one, as we are one, **23** I in them and you in me, that they may become completely one, so that the world may know that you have sent me and have loved them even as you have loved me.
24 Father, I desire that those also, whom you have given me, may be with me where I am, to see my glory, which you have given me because you loved me before the foundation of the world.

25 "Righteous Father, the world does not know you, but I know you; and these know that you have sent me. **26** I made your name known to them, and I will make it known, so that the love with which you have loved me may be in them, and I in them."

Jesus Prays for Himself (17:1–5)

Jesus' prayer comes between his final words to his disciples (often called the *Farewell Discourse*) and the beginning of his trial, crucifixion, and resurrection. He recognized that his hour had come and that all he'd been doing in his ministry was coming to a climax.

In these moments, Jesus prayed that he would be glorified. Why?

This was no selfish *give me fame* kind of prayer, for he was praying that by receiving the glory of the Father he would in turn glorify God by being obedient to the plan of redeeming the world. Jesus' prayer for glory signaled, in part, a return to his pre-existent glory. It speaks of the miraculous story of the incarnation, but it also emphasizes that Jesus would return to his former glory only through the path of obedience unto death.

However, there is more here. This prayer clearly aligns Jesus' personal will with that of the Father. The aim of this portion of the prayer is to *sync up*, as we might say, with the Father, and by way of complete obedience have the same glory in the cross that Jesus had in the presence of the Father before the world existed.

If we take a cue for our own prayer life, we see that one criteria of prayer is that our prayer requests glorify God in some way, and honor God's will with words that lead to action. A prayer for material success or personal accomplishment wilts when compared to the selfless prayer of Jesus.

Jesus Prays for His Disciples (17:6–19)

The conversation with the Father now turns to the ones with whom Jesus had shared life intimately. He prayed for his disciples, the ones who had seen his healing, learned under his teaching, and on whom would be the burden of living the faith after the resurrection.

Jesus knew what trials lay ahead for his closest followers. His prayer anticipated the martyrdom of some of the disciples. It foreshadowed the conflict between Peter and the apostles with the Jewish and Roman authorities. Jesus prayed for their protection and pleaded that God would unify them in one another in the same way that Jesus and the Father are unified.

Jesus prayed, "I have given them your word, and the world has hated them because they do not belong to the world" (John 17:14). He knew his teachings had set the disciples in opposition to the world, and this is no less true today for faithful Christians. The dominant culture is, at best, apathetic toward Christian practices and in worse scenarios at odds completely with the Christian worldview and lifestyle. Jesus' prayer raises our awareness of the challenges of living faithfully in an opposing culture.

However, removal from the world that opposes Christianity is not an option. Jesus did not pray that his disciples would be taken from the world even though Jesus knew living in such a world would be difficult for his followers. In fact, Jesus did not pray that things would be easy for his disciples. He didn't pray that God would give them an exemption from trial but instead said, "I am not asking you to take them out of the world, but I ask that you protect them from the evil one" (John 17:15).

Another cue for our prayer life lies in verse 15. Our prayer should not be for escape from our troubles. Instead, Jesus' prayer cues us to pray for protection instead of removal, for greater trust in God's word that has been given to us, and for greater faith in the power that an intimate relationship with Jesus brings.

Additionally, we do well to pray for greater intimacy and closeness with the living person of Jesus. The strength of Jesus seems to have come from his intimacy with the Father. That same kind of intimacy is accessible to modern disciples. Just like all our relationships, the strength of intimacy comes from our investment in that relationship. As Christians engage the world, there is much need for a closer walk with Jesus.

Jesus Prays for the Church (17:20–26)

Finally, Jesus' prayer turns to a third matter—for the "ones who will believe in me on behalf of their word" (17:20).

Jesus was speaking to God on behalf of the church that was yet to come. While Jesus didn't use the word *church*, church as we know it was the object of his concern, and it is comforting to hear of Jesus' love for us. The overhearing of this prayer is a tender gift akin to basking in the purest love you can imagine. The depth and breadth of Jesus' love for humankind is unveiled on the cross, and that love is found in this prayer.

Jesus anticipated that his close disciples would emerge from the wild ride of the resurrection and be passionate and vigorous in their belief in him. He knew that their passion would spread like wildfire to the others around them and that the word of the disciples would be the witness that offered firmness of faith to the early church. He also knew that difficulty would come, and such difficulty would lead to strife between his followers. He knew as well that the scandal of the cross would put all followers at odds with the world.

In that knowledge, Jesus prayed for unity that the church "may be one" (17:21). Jesus prayed first for his own glorification (17:1–5) and then for the protection of the disciples (17:6–19). Now he prayed that there may be closeness and intimacy among all followers such as there is between the Father and Jesus. "I in them and you in me," he prayed in verse 23, knowing it was going to take nothing less than the power of God to keep these ragamuffins then—and we ragamuffins now—unified and strong enough to face the trials to come.

The prayer has an evangelistic angle as well. Jesus was praying that the *unity of community* would be a signal to the world that he truly is the Son of God. This unity was to shape the identity of a counter-cultural movement that would become the church. The witness to the world is that the church would be composed of people who love one another so well that it would be clear this love had to come from a higher power. It's just not normal for people to behave with such love otherwise!

Jesus' final request of the Father was that those who believe in him "may be with me where I am, to see my glory, which you have given me because you loved me before the foundation of the world" (17:24). There are many things to appreciate in Jesus' prayer, but herein lies potentially the most exciting promise. The prayer echoes portions of John 14, where Jesus promised, "I go to prepare a place for you, and if I go and prepare a place for you, I will come again and will take you to myself . . ." (14:2b–3a).

Jesus' prayer that we may be with him is a confirmation that a great future awaits us. Jesus' love for his followers is so deep that he wants to spend all of time and eternity with us. But because of the great distance between God's holiness and humans' sinfulness, this eternal fellowship is impossible. God cannot allow sinfulness in the boundaries of heaven, and so Jesus had to take action.

Marvel at this. Ponder and wonder. Consider how great the love of Jesus must have been that he would pray for our eternal fellowship knowing that this prayer would cause him betrayal, suffering, and death. The power of life over death would be displayed, and as Jesus was victorious to the end, we see that the power of love surpasses all else.

We are challenged to pray as Jesus prayed, conforming our will to God's will despite our personal preferences. We are challenged to pray that in our own hour of trial we might live as fully as Jesus died. This prayer sees to all the details: glory for Jesus, protection for the disciples, and power and promise for the church.

Implications and Actions

When Jesus' prayer for unity is demonstrated in us, the church gives witness of God's power to the world. When we handle our disputes in humility and kindness, we are able to bear witness to the world of the power of God. When the world sees us model reconciliation with one another, we become ambassadors of God's reconciliation for all people.

John 17 inspires us to lift our hands in prayer, and it also encourages us to extend our hands to others in service, healing, and forgiveness. Jesus prayed for us to be unified, but churches are still filled with conflict. Jesus prayed that the love of the Father would be in us, but sometimes we don't have very much love for ourselves or for others.

What is the church to do? You and your church simply *must* find ways to love one another, even when you don't feel like it. Our churches must rely on the power of prayer in this matter, praying continually when there is conflict, and even when there is not. Let this movement begin by practicing love for one another beginning with your study group. Then imagine and implement practical ways in which your group's practice of love can branch out to your church and beyond.

KOINONIA

Koinonia is a Greek word that sometimes gets bandied about in the church without full understanding. We know it means *fellowship*, but what is this fellowship like?

George R. Beasley-Murray, a New Testament scholar, suggested that Jesus' prayer that "they also be in us" (John 17:21) is the profound goal of fellowship. The church gains unity by enjoying the fellowship between the Father and the Son, and that unity, when duplicated among and between Jesus' followers, makes *koinonia* live.[1]

A unified church with good fellowship is made up of members who

- Pray for one another as Jesus prayed for us

- Endeavor to be in fellowship with God through practicing spiritual disciplines

- Work for love in the community of faith by focusing on others' needs

- Consider themselves to be bearers of Jesus' love and grace to others by adopting a servant attitude

WHAT FELLOWSHIP MEANS

The third part of Jesus' prayer for his followers shows how followers of Jesus should pray for one another (John 17:20–26). It also forms the basis for how we *do* fellowship.

Growing up in church in the South, I simply thought *fellowship* was the title of an event, like a potluck supper or dinner on the grounds. But, later in life, I learned that fellowship is better defined as loving one another as Jesus loves us.

Looking at Jesus' prayer, what clues do you have about how Jesus loves you? Once you answer that, the harder question surfaces: Can you love your fellow believers in the same way? How?

QUESTIONS

1. For whom did Jesus pray?

2. What are three or four words to describe how Jesus prayed?

3. How does Jesus' prayer portray his relationship with the Father?

4. What does Jesus' prayer teach you about Jesus' nature?

5. How does it affect you to know that Jesus prayed long ago for your church?

6. How does Jesus' prayer affect your thinking about conflict within your church? Does it, for example, encourage and inspire you to work toward healthy conflict resolution?

7. How could Jesus' prayer in John 17 influence the way you pray? What kinds of things did Jesus ask God to do? What kinds of things do you ask of God?

8. Given that Jesus prayed for us in his final hours before the crucifixion, how should you pray when faced with trials and hardships?

9. What are two or three things you learn from John 17 about the practice of prayer?

NOTES ————————————————————————————————

1. George R. Beasley-Murray, "The Community of True Life," *Review and Expositor*, vol. 85, no. 3, 1988, pp. 482–483.

Jesus' Trial and Crucifixion

Unit two of the study of *Part Two—The Light Overcomes (John 13—21)* deals with Scripture selections from John 18—19. The two lessons in this unit are on Jesus' trial and crucifixion.[1]

Lesson six (John 18:15–27; 18:33—19:16) looks at the ways in which the Jewish leaders, Peter, and Pilate responded under pressure when faced with a decision about Jesus at his trial. The Scripture passages show the need for disciples to remain faithful to Jesus even under pressure and for all people to make the right decision about Jesus.

Lesson seven (John 19:16b–30, 38–42) focuses on Jesus' crucifixion. The lesson calls for a response to the meaning of Jesus' crucifixion.

N O T E S

1. Unless otherwise indicated, all Scripture quotations in unit two, lessons six and seven, are from the New American Standard Bible (1995 update).

LESSON SIX

Judging Jesus

MAIN IDEA

Jesus' identity as God's Son challenges each person with a choice about him.

QUESTION TO EXPLORE

What judgment do you make about Jesus?

STUDY AIM

To identify how each main character in Jesus' trials responded to Jesus and to testify of my faith in Jesus as God's Son in spite of pressures I face

QUICK READ

Peter was prepared to lay down his life for Jesus. Yet in the most crucial hour he denied knowing Christ. How do we respond to Jesus when our own personal interests and even safety are at risk?

Jesus faced unbelievably intense pressure as he stood before Annas and Caiaphas, the religious leaders, and then before Pilate, Rome's governor. Gone were the crowd's shouts of "Hosanna!" at the beginning of Holy Week (John 12:13). Religious leaders who pretended to love God and political leaders who were sworn to serve Caesar followed their own selfish ambitions and sought to extinguish the Light that exposed their darkness. Jesus was unwavering, courageous, and unafraid of their verdict. However, the others involved in this historic scene revealed personal fears, ambitions, and animosity.

We are tempted to read the Gospel accounts of Judas's betrayal, Peter's denial, the crowd's hostility, and the political and religious leaders' injustice, and condemn these acts. Yet when we put ourselves in their situation, we are faced with the question of what our response would have been.

JOHN 18:15–27, 33–40

15 Simon Peter was following Jesus, and so was another disciple. Now that disciple was known to the high priest, and entered with Jesus into the court of the high priest, **16** but Peter was standing at the door outside. So the other disciple, who was known to the high priest, went out and spoke to the doorkeeper, and brought Peter in. **17** Then the slave-girl who kept the door said to Peter, "You are not also one of this man's disciples, are you?" He said, "I am not." **18** Now the slaves and the officers were standing there, having made a charcoal fire, for it was cold and they were warming themselves; and Peter was also with them, standing and warming himself. **19** The high priest then questioned Jesus about His disciples, and about His teaching. **20** Jesus answered him, "I have spoken openly to the world; I always taught in synagogues and in the temple, where all the Jews come together; and I spoke nothing in secret. **21** "Why do you question Me? Question those who have heard what I spoke to them; they know what I said." **22** When He had said this, one of the officers standing nearby struck Jesus, saying, "Is that the way You answer the high priest?" **23** Jesus answered him, "If I have spoken wrongly, testify of the wrong; but if rightly, why do you strike Me?" **24** So Annas sent Him bound to Caiaphas the high priest. **25** Now Simon Peter was standing and warming himself. So they said to him, "You are not also one of His disciples, are you?" He denied it, and said, "I am not." **26** One of the slaves of the high priest, being a relative of the one whose ear Peter cut off, said, "Did I not see you in the garden with Him?" **27** Peter then denied it again, and immediately a rooster crowed.

• •

33 Therefore Pilate entered again into the Praetorium, and summoned Jesus and said to Him, "Are You the King of the Jews?" **34** Jesus answered, "Are you saying this on your own initiative, or did others tell you about Me?" **35** Pilate answered, "I am not a Jew, am I? Your own nation and the chief priests delivered You to me; what have You done?" **36** Jesus answered, "My kingdom is not of this world. If My kingdom were of this world, then My servants would be fighting so that I would not be handed over to the Jews; but as it is, My kingdom is not of this realm." **37** Therefore Pilate said to Him, "So You are a king?" Jesus answered, "You say correctly that I am a king. For this I have been born, and for this I have come into the world, to testify to the truth. Everyone who is of the truth hears My voice." **38** Pilate said to Him, "What is truth?" And when he had said this, he went out again to the Jews and said to them, "I find no guilt in Him. **39** "But you have a custom that I release someone for you at the Passover; do you wish then that I release for you the King of the Jews?" **40** So they cried out again, saying, "Not this Man, but Barabbas." Now Barabbas was a robber.

JOHN 19:1–16

1 Pilate then took Jesus and scourged Him. **2** And the soldiers twisted together a crown of thorns and put it on His head, and put a purple robe on Him; **3** and they began to come up to Him and say, "Hail, King of the Jews!" and to give Him slaps in the face. **4** Pilate came out again and said to them, "Behold, I am bringing Him out to you so that you may know that I find no guilt in Him." **5** Jesus then came out, wearing the crown of thorns and the purple robe. Pilate said to them, "Behold, the Man!" **6** So when the chief priests and the officers saw Him, they cried out saying, "Crucify, crucify!" Pilate said to them, "Take Him yourselves and crucify Him, for I find no guilt in Him." **7** The Jews answered him, "We have a law, and by that law He ought to die because He made Himself out to be the Son of God." **8** Therefore when Pilate heard this statement, he was even more afraid; **9** and he entered into the Praetorium again and said to Jesus, "Where are You from?" But Jesus gave him no answer. **10** So Pilate said to Him, "You do not speak to me? Do You not know that I have authority to release You, and I have authority to crucify You?" **11** Jesus answered, "You would have no authority over Me, unless it had been given you from above; for this reason he who delivered Me to you has the greater sin." **12** As a result of this Pilate made efforts to release Him, but the Jews cried out saying, "If you release this Man, you are no friend of Caesar; everyone who makes himself out to be a king opposes Caesar." **13** Therefore when Pilate heard these words, he brought Jesus out, and sat down on the judgment seat at a place called The Pavement, but in Hebrew, Gabbatha. **14** Now it was the day of preparation for the Passover; it was about the sixth hour. And he said to the Jews, "Behold, your King!" **15** So they cried out, "Away with Him, away with Him, crucify Him!" Pilate said to them, "Shall I crucify your King?" The chief priests answered, "We have no king but Caesar." **16** So he then handed Him over to them to be crucified.

The Greed of Judas (18:1–14)

Jesus spent significant time in prayer before major events, and so it was not unusual that he would go to a familiar place of prayer, Gethsemane, on the night of his arrest. Judas and all the disciples knew the place well. On that night Judas led a cohort of soldiers and officials from the chief priests and Pharisees to arrest Jesus.

Jesus knew all the things that were coming upon him (John 18:4). He had already predicted Judas's betrayal and Peter's denial. He knew the mockery, abuse, pain, and shame that awaited him. Yet he went boldly to the soldiers and announced "I am He" (18:5). The very "I Am" who spoke this name to Moses was now about to deliver himself over to be killed by the ones he created.[1] The cohort drew back and fell to the ground. One day everyone will fall before Jesus and every tongue will confess that Jesus is Lord (Philippians 2:11).

Peter drew his sword courageously to fight off the enemy. A short time later that courage abandoned him.

There are many speculations about why Judas would betray Jesus. The most obvious is greed. He sold Jesus for a few coins. He was also the treasurer for the disciples and stole from the money box (John 12:4–6). Unfortunately Judas would not be the last one who turned away from Jesus for material gain.

The Fear of Peter (18:15–18)

Jesus was arrested and bound. Then he was brought first to Annas, the father-in-law of Caiaphas, the high priest that year.

Unlike the other disciples who scattered, Peter and an unnamed disciple followed Jesus. Many speculate that John, the author of this Gospel, was the other person because of his eyewitness account. The other disciple was known by the high priest and entered the court of the high priest, but Peter stood at the door outside. "Then the slave-girl who kept the door said to Peter, 'You are not also one of this man's disciples, are you?' He said, 'I am not'" (John 18:17).

Peter had said just hours earlier he would lay down his life for Jesus (13:37). Jesus warned him that he would deny him three times before the rooster crowed (13:38). Peter bravely defended Jesus in the garden and followed Jesus to the high priest's house. Yet for some reason he was unwilling to admit being one of Jesus' followers when confronted by a "servant-girl" (Luke 22:56).

We are warned in 1 Corinthians 10:12, "Therefore let him who thinks he stands take heed that he does not fall." Peter may have been reminded of this situation when he wrote, "Be of sober spirit, be on the alert. Your adversary, the devil, prowls around like a roaring lion, seeking someone to devour" (1 Peter 5:8). Perhaps if Peter had stayed awake and prayed in the garden with Jesus he would have found the courage to stand strong.

How many times have we disappointed Christ and others by failing to speak when we should have, or have failed to take a stand for justice when the mood of the crowd was against us?

The Hypocrisy of the High Priests (18:19–24)

The Fourth Gospel is the only one that mentions Jesus' trial before Annas. Annas was obviously an influential person, having been high priest A.D. 6–15. At least five of his sons and one grandson also became high priests. Caiaphas, the high priest at the time of Jesus' arrest, was his son-in-law. There must have been an arrangement that Jesus would be brought first to Annas.

This was more like a police interrogation than a trial, for many of the normal rights of prisoners were overlooked. Jesus called for Annas to question those who heard him speak, which was one of Jesus' rights as a prisoner. In a cowardly way, one of the officials struck Jesus, who was still bound. Annas then sent Jesus to Caiaphas.

While priests were killing the Passover lambs, the high priest, who was supposed to represent God to his people, taunted the Lamb of God. The actions of the religious leaders remind us that not everyone who speaks for

God knows God. Some of the most atrocious acts of cruelty, including the crucifixion of Jesus, have been done in the name of God. Some of Jesus' strongest rebukes were leveled at the religious leaders (Matthew 23; John 19:11). The prophet Ezekiel scolded the shepherds who fed themselves and not the flocks (Ezekiel 34:8). We should test the words of preachers by the Word of God and test the authenticity of their lives by the fruit of the Spirit.

The Denial of Peter (18:25–27)

Unfortunately Peter continued to deny knowing Christ even to a relative of Malchus, whose ear Peter had severed. Chrysostom, the gifted fourth-century Christian preacher, spoke of how this once "hot and furious" disciple "was now lethargic when Jesus was being led away! After such things as had taken place, he does not move but still warms himself. This happened so that you might learn how great the weakness of our nature is if God abandons us. And, being questioned, he denies again."[2]

The Insecurity of Pilate (18:28–38)

Jesus was led from Caiaphas to the praetorium, the governor's official residence. The Jews continued their hypocrisy by refusing to go inside the residence so they wouldn't be defiled and unable to eat the Passover meal. This tradition came from Jewish teachings that a Gentile's home was unclean. Baptist New Testament scholar George Beasley-Murray stated, "No more eloquent example than this can be found of the ability of religious people to be meticulous about external regulations of religion while being wholly at variance with God."[3]

Pilate questioned the religious leaders about their accusation against Jesus and instructed them to judge him according to their law. They responded that they had no authority to put him to death.

The stoning of Stephen would later prove this statement incorrect. However, the Jewish leaders wanted Jesus crucified, which only the Roman leader could sanction. The Jews wanted to make a spectacle of his death. Stoning might have made him a martyr. Jesus did not come to die as a martyr but as a ransom. "Anyone who is hung on a tree is under God's curse" (Deuteronomy 21:23, NIV). Jesus took the curse of sin upon himself.

Pilate asked Jesus whether he was "the King of the Jews" (John 18:33). Jesus questioned Pilate as to whether he was asking this of himself or from others. Pilate declared he was no Jew and that the Jewish leaders had offered up Jesus. "Jesus answered, 'My Kingdom is not of this world. If My Kingdom were of this world, then My servants would be fighting . . .'" (John 18:36).

As Pilate and Jesus continued to converse about Jesus' kingship, Pilate said to Jesus, "So You are a king?" Jesus replied, "You say correctly that I am a king. For this I have been born, and for this I have come into the world, to testify to the truth. Everyone who is of the truth hears My voice" (18:37). Pilate responded with his now-famous question, "What is truth?" (18:38). Pilate's conversation with Jesus ended there.

Pilate obviously knew Jesus was innocent of all charges. He saw the jealousy of the leaders. He had the political authority to make the right call and free Jesus. Yet his insecurity and his fear of Caesar and of the people caused him to compromise the truth for political gain.

How many kingdom opportunities are lost because we are more concerned about the opinions of others than about the truth? Pilate stood before the one who is the truth and yet missed out on eternal life because of his concern for worldly approval. What a high price to pay for the fickle affirmation of others!

The Freedom of Barabbas (18:39–40)

Pilate declared that Jesus was innocent. He gave the people an opportunity to release Jesus by invoking the custom of releasing a prisoner at Passover. He offered them the King of the Jews or Barabbas. They cried for Barabbas.

We know little about Barabbas. In John's Gospel he is described as a robber. In Mark 15:7 he is said to be an insurrectionist who committed murder in the uprising.

The people asked for the release of a notorious prisoner instead of the innocent Jesus.

Barabbas is an example of one who is guilty being freed by the substitution of Jesus. Jesus' vicarious death still provides freedom to those who trust him.

The Hostility of the People (19:1–16)

Jesus was handed over to the soldiers to be scourged. Whips used in such a scourging would include spikes or bones joined together. In the scourging, flesh was torn from the victims. They often collapsed or even died under this treatment. It was amazing that Jesus could walk afterwards. There is no wonder that he fell under the weight of the cross.

The soldiers ridiculed Jesus, anointing him with a painful crown of thorns and giving him a purple robe. They slapped him and cried, "Hail, King of the Jews!" (John 19:3).

The pitiful sight of one who had been so abused failed to bring sympathy from the crowds. They continued to cry for his crucifixion, claiming, "He made Himself out to be the Son of God" (John 19:7).

Pilate became more afraid and asked Jesus where he was from. Jesus gave no answer. Pilate reminded Jesus that he had the power to release him or crucify him. Jesus said Pilate would have no authority unless it had been granted from above.

The crowds threatened Pilate with his loyalty to Caesar. Pilate capitulated and offered them Jesus. Pilate asked, "Shall I crucify your King?" The chief priests responded, "We have no king but Caesar" (19:15).

The brutality of humanity is one of the clearest proofs of the reality of evil. The atrocities committed against Jesus reveal the heart of humankind that continues to torture those who stand in the way of personal goals and agendas.

Implications for Life

As Jesus moves closer to the cross in the Gospel of John, we see a clearer picture of the awesomeness of God's love and the awfulness of human sin. Jesus had come to give his life as a ransom. Nothing deterred him from this assignment. Jesus faced the betrayal of an associate, the denial of a friend, the hypocrisy of those who supposedly spoke for God, and the brutality of one of the most painful executions ever invented. He never backed down. He stood with courage, humility, and compassion.

Jesus provided a distinctive contrast to the greed, fear, insecurity, and hostility of those around him. John's Gospel gives a clear picture of a world desperately in need of a Savior.

THE HISTORY OF THE HIGH PRIEST

The high priest was originally appointed for life and came from the priestly family. During the Hellenistic Period (333–70 B.C.), the priesthood led the nation. The head of the temple, the high priest, was the de facto leader of the government of Judea. He represented Judea to the ruling leaders, collected taxes, and was responsible for the spiritual welfare of the people.

Until the time of Antiochus Epiphanes (175–163 B.C.), the high priest held the office for life. When Herod became king in 37 B.C., the rule of the nation shifted from priests to a secular monarchy. Herod appointed the priests and reduced them to a ceremonial role. During the time of Jesus, the Roman procurators appointed the high priests, many of whom bought their office through their great wealth.

APPLICATIONS

- I will meditate on this passage for seven days and focus on Christ's love for me and my desperate need for him.

- I will lead my family to pray together this week, giving thanks for Christ's redemptive work.

- I will join with other Christians to begin a new ministry that shares the love of Christ with a family who has been victimized by injustice.

- I will encourage my church to share the hope of Christ with a nearby community that is largely unreached.

QUESTIONS

1. What do Jesus' actions show you about God?

2. What do Jesus' actions tell you about the human condition?

3. In what ways can greed keep us from knowing God's plan for our lives?

4. When has fear robbed you of an opportunity to stand up for what is right?

5. Why do we allow the opinions of others to dictate our actions?

6. What are some examples of brutality that have been done in the name of God (including Christianity)?

NOTES

1. See Exodus 3:14.

2. Chrysostom, *Homilies on the Gospel of John*, 83.3. See http://www. ccel.org/ccel/schaff/npnf114.iv.lxxxv.html.

3. George R. Beasley-Murray, *John,* Word Biblical Commentary, vol. 36 (Waco, Texas: Word Books, Publisher, 1987), 328.

FOCAL TEXT
John 19:16b–30, 38–42

BACKGROUND
John 19:16b–42

LESSON SEVEN
Dying to Bring Life

MAIN IDEA

Jesus' sacrifice of himself on the cross brings life to all who will turn to him.

QUESTION TO EXPLORE

What was "finished" at Jesus' cross?

STUDY AIM

To trace the events of Jesus' crucifixion and to determine how I will respond to its meaning

QUICK READ

Jesus came to give his life as a ransom (Mark 10:45). He accomplished this with his death on the cross. Now Jesus offers life to all who call on him.

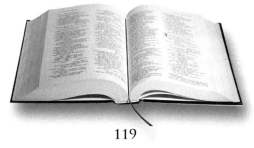

What is your defining hour? Patrick Henry's may have come when he said, "Give me liberty or give me death." John Kennedy spoke memorable words when he said, "Ask not what your country can do for you—ask what you can do for your country." Martin Luther King's purpose may have been best articulated when he announced, "I have a dream." In this passage, Jesus' hour had come.

JOHN 19:16B–30, 38–42

17 They took Jesus, therefore, and He went out, bearing His own cross, to the place called the Place of a Skull, which is called in Hebrew, Golgotha. **18** There they crucified Him, and with Him two other men, one on either side, and Jesus in between. **19** Pilate also wrote an inscription and put it on the cross. It was written, "JESUS THE NAZARENE, THE KING OF THE JEWS." **20** Therefore many of the Jews read this inscription, for the place where Jesus was crucified was near the city; and it was written in Hebrew, Latin and in Greek. **21** So the chief priests of the Jews were saying to Pilate, "Do not write, 'The King of the Jews'; but that He said, 'I am King of the Jews.'" **22** Pilate answered, "What I have written I have written." **23** Then the soldiers, when they had crucified Jesus, took His outer garments and made four parts, a part to every soldier and also the tunic; now the tunic was seamless, woven in one piece. **24** So they said to one another, "Let us not tear it, but cast lots for it, to decide whose it shall be"; this was to fulfill the Scripture:, "They divided My outer garments among them, and for My clothing they cast lots." **25** Therefore the soldiers did these things. But standing by the cross of Jesus were His mother, and His mother's sister, Mary the wife of Clopas, and Mary Magdalene. **26** When Jesus then saw His mother, and the disciple whom He loved standing nearby, He said to His mother, "Woman, behold, your son!" **27** Then He said to the disciple, "Behold, your mother!" From that hour the disciple took her into his own household. **28** After this, Jesus, knowing that all things had already been accomplished, to fulfill the Scripture, said, "I am thirsty." **29** A jar full of sour wine was standing there; so they put a sponge full of the sour wine upon a branch of hyssop and brought it up to His mouth. **30** Therefore when Jesus had received the sour wine, He said, "It is finished!" And He bowed His head and gave up His spirit.

• •

38 After these things Joseph of Arimathea, being a disciple of Jesus, but a secret one for fear of the Jews, asked Pilate that he might take away the body of Jesus; and Pilate granted permission. So he came and took away His body. **39** Nicodemus, who had first come to Him by night, also came, bringing a mixture of myrrh and aloes, about a hundred pounds weight. **40** So they took the body of Jesus and bound it in linen wrappings with the spices, as is the burial custom of the Jews. **41** Now in the place where

He was crucified there was a garden, and in the garden a new tomb in which no one had yet been laid. **42** Therefore because of the Jewish day of preparation, since the tomb was nearby, they laid Jesus there.

Jesus' Hour Has Come

Jesus' ministry was to die on the cross as a ransom for our sins. He was a teacher, a moral example, a compassionate healer, and an inspirational leader. Yet none of these was his primary task. Jesus had an appointment with the cross, and nothing distracted him from that assignment.

Jesus referred to the hour of his suffering throughout the Gospel of John. At the wedding in Cana when Jesus performed his first miracle, he said, "My hour has not yet come" (John 2:4). When Jesus fed the multitude and perceived they wanted to make him king, he withdrew from the crowds (6:15).

When Jesus' brothers urged him to go to the Festival of Booths in Jerusalem, he said, "My time is not yet here" (7:6, 8). Later Jesus came to Jerusalem. There he announced, "I am the Light of the world" (8:12). Yet "no one seized Him, because his hour had not yet come" (8:20).

However in John 12:23, Jesus told Andrew and Philip, "The hour has come for the Son of Man to be glorified." He went on, "My soul has become troubled; and what shall I say, 'Father, save Me from this hour'? But for this purpose I came to this hour" (12:27). When Jesus met with the disciples before the Feast of the Passover, he knew that his hour had come (13:1). In Jesus' priestly prayer, he said, "Father, the hour has come; glorify Your Son, that the Son may glorify You" (17:1).

Jesus knew his destiny was death because of the hostility of the Jewish leaders and because of the prophecies of Scripture. Yet, primarily because of his deliberate choice, he let nothing deter him from the cross. He had come to seek and save the lost (Luke 19:10).[1]

Jesus Bears His Cross (19:16–24)

The Gospel of John gives few details about Jesus' crucifixion. It simply states that Pilate handed Jesus over to be crucified. The account of Jesus' death follows historical accounts of crucifixion. As New Testament commentator William Barclay states, "There was no more terrible death than death by crucifixion. Even the Romans themselves regarded it with a shudder of horror. Cicero declared that it was 'the most cruel and horrifying death.' Tacitus said that it was a 'despicable death.' . . . It was that death, the most dreaded death in the ancient world, the death of slaves and criminals that Jesus died."[2]

It was common for the victim to carry the crossbeam to the place of execution where the upright was already in place. Some believe Jesus may have carried the entire cross. Romans paraded the victims through the streets as a reminder to the crowds that Rome would not tolerate their crimes. Like Isaac carrying the wood for his own sacrifice, Jesus went through the crowded streets, beaten and bloodied. He came to the place of the Skull, Golgotha, in Hebrew, or Calvary, in Latin, where he was nailed to the cross.

The kind of cross used in that day could be in the shape of an *X* or a *T*. Since the title was placed over Jesus' head, the *T*-shaped cross would have been what was used. The nails were five to seven inches long and driven through the wrists and feet. Usually the person was only a short distance from the ground, although Jesus must have been elevated some because a stick was needed to offer him a drink. The nails caused a great deal of bleeding, but death usually came from suffocation.[3]

According to the custom, an inscription announced the crime that had been committed. "Pilate also wrote an inscription and put it on the cross. It was written, 'JESUS THE NAZARENE, THE KING OF THE JEWS'" (19:19). "NAZARENE" revealed Jesus' humble roots at Nazareth, and "KING" described his exalted position.

The Jews were angry with Pilate and asked that the title be amended that Jesus "said" he was the king of the Jews. For once, Pilate stood firm before them and let what was written stand.

The psalmist prophesied, "They divide my garments among them, and for my clothing they cast lots"

(Psalm 22:18). The four soldiers who had escorted Jesus to the cross divided Jesus' outer garments, each receiving one article. Yet rather than tearing the seamless tunic, they cast lots to see who would receive it.

Some have spoken of the seamless tunic as identification with the high priest's robe or the unity of the new Christian community Jesus had established. It is hard to support either of these ideas. However, as William Barclay states, "There is no picture which so shows the indifference of the world to Christ. There, on the Cross, Jesus was dying in agony; and there at the foot of the Cross the soldiers threw their dice as if it did not matter."[4] It is hard to imagine which is greater, the brutality of Jesus' opponents or the indifference of the world to Christ's redemptive love.

Jesus' Final Hour (19:25–30)

Jesus' divinity and humanity were both clearly seen at the cross. While he was fulfilling his kingdom assignment as a ransom for the whole world, he still cared for his earthly mother. Jesus looked down on Mary, standing near with her friends, and said to "the disciple whom He loved . . . 'Behold, your mother!' From that hour the disciple took her into his own household" (John 19:26–27).

The incident shows that Jesus, the firstborn son of Mary, still had a son's love for his mother, even while he also loved the whole world. He didn't neglect earthly responsibilities while performing heavenly tasks.

Jesus' humanity was also revealed when he cried out, "I am thirsty" (19:28). This statement may have spiritual meaning related to Jesus' word in the garden that he must drink the cup the Father had given him (18:11). Yet we shouldn't forget Jesus' human anguish. There is no indication Jesus had drunk anything since the meal with his disciples. He had traveled to the garden to pray. Then he had been arrested and tried before Annas, Caiaphas, Pilate, and Herod. He then had been brutally beaten and nailed to the cross. Jesus' thirst was just another manifestation of his suffering.

Jesus had earlier rejected the wine mixed with myrrh (Mark 15:23), which was prepared to dull the senses and lessen the pain. However, he received the vinegar offered him just as the psalmist had prophesied, "And for my thirst they gave me vinegar to drink" (Ps. 69:21).

Just as the blood of the Passover lambs was sprinkled with a hyssop branch over the doorposts of the Hebrews as they observed Passover, Jesus was offered sour wine hoisted to him with a hyssop branch. Thus Jesus himself was the Passover Lamb who takes away the sin of the world.

"Therefore when Jesus had received the sour wine, He said, 'It is finished!' And He bowed His head and gave up His spirit" (John 19:30). The ordeal of the crucifixion was finished. His hour was accomplished. The price of the ransom was *paid in full*!

The Romans customarily left the victims on the cross for days until they died. Victims of crucifixion often died a slow and painful death. Vultures would tear off their flesh. The bodies would then just be cast aside. Yet with the Sabbath and the Passover approaching, the Jewish leaders wanted Jesus' body off the cross. So they asked Pilate to break his legs to hasten his death. Breaking the legs hastened death through loss of blood and suffocation.[5] Suffocation resulted because the victim could not support his body with his broken legs.

When the soldiers saw that Jesus was already dead, they didn't break his legs, however. This decision fulfilled the Scripture, "Not a bone of Him shall be broken" (19:36). "One of the soldiers pierced His side with a spear, and immediately blood and water came forth" (19:34).

Various explanations have been given for the flow of blood and water from Jesus' body at this point. Among the most common are that the scourging had caused blood to accumulate in Jesus' chest and it flowed out when he was pierced. Another is that the spear pierced Jesus' heart, resulting in water coming from the sac around the heart.[6] Spiritual speculation has been offered that the water and blood symbolized the ordinances of baptism and communion. The primary purpose for the Gospel of John mentioning this incident, though, is that it is proof of the physical death of Jesus. "And he who has seen has testified, and his testimony is true; and he knows that he is telling the truth, so that you also may believe" (19:35).

Jesus' Secret Disciples (19:38–42)

Joseph of Arimathea is identified in the other Gospels as a wealthy member of the Sanhedrin (see Matthew 27:57–60; Mark 15:43–46; Luke 23:50–53). Nicodemus, also a member of the Sanhedrin, was not publicly identified with Jesus but had visited Jesus at night (see John 3:1–10; 7:50). The Gospel of John describes Joseph as a secret disciple of Jesus who kept his loyalty private because of his fear of the Jews. Joseph, and presumably Nicodemus, had not voted with the rest of the Sanhedrin to execute Jesus and took pity on Jesus at his death. Their show of love for Jesus at his death by providing for his burial showed great courage, especially since it would have appeared at that point that Jesus' movement was over. Their act identified them publicly with Jesus. The staggering amount of spices Nicodemus brought was consistent with gifts for royal funerals.

Joseph's brave request and Nicodemus's generous provision indicate a new relationship between these men and Jesus. Jesus was lifted up on the cross, and they are examples of those who are drawn to him.

"It Is Finished!"

When Jesus said, "It is finished!" he announced the end to his suffering, but also much more. Jesus' hour had been accomplished. His purpose for coming to the world to give his life as a ransom was complete. His sinless life and his vicarious death had paid the terrible price for the "wages of sin" (Romans 6:23).

When a mortgage has been paid off the note is stamped, *Paid in Full!* When Jesus cried out, "It is finished!" he was saying our sin debt was *Paid in Full.*

"My sin, oh, the bliss of this glorious thought! My sin not in part, but the whole is nailed to the cross, and I bear it no more, Praise the Lord, praise the Lord, O my soul!"[7]

JESUS' FRIENDS AT THE CROSS (19:25–27)

The Gospel of Mark mentions three women who were standing at a distance when Jesus was crucified, including Mary Magdalene, Mary the mother of James the Less and Joses, and Salome (Mark 15:40). The Gospel of John speaks of four who were standing near the cross. Perhaps the women drew nearer as the soldiers moved away and as Jesus' death approached. The assumption has long been held that Mary the wife of Clopas is Mary the mother of James the Less and Joses, and also that Salome is Jesus' mother's sister and the mother of the sons of Zebedee.[8]

What a strange entourage at Jesus' death. We don't know anything about Mary the wife of Clopas, but we do know the others. Jesus had cast seven demons form Mary Magdalene (Luke 8:2). The mother of James and John was the one Jesus rebuked for asking for prestigious positions for her sons in Jesus' kingdom. Then of course the other one was Jesus' mother. No person is too good or too evil to turn to Jesus on the cross.

APPLICATIONS

- What does Jesus' death on the cross mean to you personally?

- What does Jesus' death say about all the peoples of the world?

- How does Jesus' death make a difference in your life?

- What modern individuals would reflect the diversity of the four women standing near Jesus on the cross?

QUESTIONS

1. What were the physical challenges Jesus faced on the cross?

2. How did Jesus' death fulfill Old Testament prophecies?

3. What was the spiritual agony Jesus suffered?

4. How does Jesus' care for Mary, while he was still on the cross, apply to priorities in your life related to your kingdom assignment and earthly responsibilities?

5. Can you picture all of your sins, past and present, nailed to the cross with Jesus?

6. Have you received Jesus' gift of eternal life as a free to gift to you?

NOTES

1. John R. W. Stott, *The Cross of Christ* (Intervarsity Press, 1986), 28.

2. William Barclay, *The Gospel of John*, vol. 2, The Daily Study Bible (Philadelphia: The Westminster Press, 1975), 250.

3. Rodney A. Whitacre, *John*, The IVP New Testament Commentary Series (Downers Grove, Illinois: InterVarsity Press, 1999), 457

4. Barclay, 254.

5. George R. Beasley-Murray, *John*, Word Biblical Commentary, vol. 36 (Waco, Texas: Word Books, Publisher, 1987), 353.

6. Whitacre, 465.

7. "It is Well With My Soul," words by Horatio G. Spafford, 1828–1888.

8. Whitacre, 460.

——— U N I T   T H R E E ———
Jesus' Resurrection

Unit three of the study of *Part Two—The Light Overcomes (John 13—21)* of the Gospel of John consists of four lessons. Each lesson deals with one of the four resurrection appearances of Jesus in John 20—21.[1] The lessons call us to affirm the reality of Jesus' resurrection and challenge us to respond to Jesus in faith and fullness of service.

NOTES ————————————————————

1. Unless otherwise indicated, all Scripture quotations in unit three, lessons eight through eleven, are from the New International Version.

133

LESSON EIGHT

Good News About Jesus

MAIN IDEA

Jesus' resurrection confirmed his identity and mission as God's Son and calls us to follow him and tell others about him.

QUESTION TO EXPLORE

To whom does Jesus wish you to go to tell good news about him?

STUDY AIM

To describe Mary Magdalene's encounter with the risen Jesus and to decide how I will tell the good news about Jesus

QUICK READ

A grieving Mary Magdalene was the first person to see the risen Lord in the Gospel of John and tell the good news of resurrection.

Cemeteries are more than burial spots. They are significant places where families go to remember loved ones and sometimes to mark birthdays or anniversaries with flowers. These places provide physical memorials that say, *These lives mattered.*

Easter combines the emotions of a cemetery with the empty tomb of a risen Lord. Families who have lost loved ones during the year are especially aware of memories of their beloved and of the resurrection hope of Christ.

Easter is not only a day to visit the tomb but also an opportunity to rekindle Christ's resurrection hope. This was certainly the case for the first person who saw Jesus after his resurrection. Mary Magdalene journeyed from being a grieving student to becoming a resurrection witness to the disciples.

John 20 traces four stages of Mary's growth as a disciple. In each stage, Mary responded to what she saw and felt; these responses moved her forward in her journey as a disciple. This lesson invites us to join her on that journey. On Easter, we come to the tomb, like Mary Magdalene, hoping to relive memories, but we return home ready to share good news.

JOHN 20:1–18

¹ Early on the first day of the week, while it was still dark, Mary Magdalene went to the tomb and saw that the stone

had been removed from the entrance. **2** So she came running to Simon Peter and the other disciple, the one Jesus loved, and said, "They have taken the Lord out of the tomb, and we don't know where they have put him!"

3 So Peter and the other disciple started for the tomb. **4** Both were running, but the other disciple outran Peter and reached the tomb first. **5** He bent over and looked in at the strips of linen lying there but did not go in. **6** Then Simon Peter, who was behind him, arrived and went into the tomb. He saw the strips of linen lying there, **7** as well as the burial cloth that had been around Jesus' head. The cloth was folded up by itself, separate from the linen. **8** Finally the other disciple, who had reached the tomb first, also went inside. He saw and believed. **9** (They still did not understand from Scripture that Jesus had to rise from the dead.)

10 Then the disciples went back to their homes, **11** but Mary stood outside the tomb crying. As she wept, she bent over to look into the tomb **12** and saw two angels in white, seated where Jesus' body had been, one at the head and the other at the foot.

13 They asked her, "Woman, why are you crying?"

"They have taken my Lord away," she said, "and I don't know where they have put him." **14** At this, she turned around and saw Jesus standing there, but she did not realize that it was Jesus.

15 "Woman," he said, "why are you crying? Who is it you are looking for?"

Thinking he was the gardener, she said, "Sir, if you have carried him away, tell me where you have put him, and I will get him."

¹⁶ Jesus said to her, "Mary."

She turned toward him and cried out in Aramaic, "Rabboni!" (which means Teacher).

¹⁷ Jesus said, "Do not hold on to me, for I have not yet returned to the Father. Go instead to my brothers and tell them, 'I am returning to my Father and your Father, to my God and your God.'"

¹⁸ Mary Magdalene went to the disciples with the news: "I have seen the Lord!" And she told them that he had said these things to her.

Visit the Tomb (20:1–2)

John's account of the resurrection traces the faith development of a woman likely from the village of Migdol, known in the New Testament as "Magdala." The village was probably located in the region of Gadara, site of the famous healing of a man with demons (Matthew 8:28–33). Jesus encountered believing Gentiles for the first time in that place. We do not know whether Mary was a Gentile; but we do know that she, like the Gadarene demoniac, was afflicted with demons (Luke 8:2).

In stage one of her faith-journey, she visited the tomb as part of the ritual burial process. Funeral homes and morticians provide for modern people what family and close friends did in the first century. In Jesus' day, people buried loved ones in caves cut from cliffs in the area. Families cared for their deceased loved ones through a series of rituals that were practical, memorable, and spiritual.

Jewish people preferred to bury loved ones within twenty-four hours of death. They placed the bodies in the cave on a bench in the middle, rolled a stone or boulder over the entrance, placed a rock to hold the boulder in position, and returned the next day to complete the cleansing ritual. The following day, mourners removed the rock holding the large stone, rolled the stone away, washed the body, and covered the deceased with spices. For a death on the day prior to the Sabbath, Friday afternoon, the body remained in the cave for two nights. Mourners returned early on the first day of the week (Sunday morning) to complete the bathing process so that the body would not stink. Most bodies decomposed within one year. On the first anniversary of death, the family members placed their bones in an ossuary (bone box) on a shelf in the family burial site inside the cave. The ritual was then complete.

In keeping with Jewish custom, Mary was the first to arrive at the tomb early Sunday morning to perform the ritual act of preparing the dead body. When Mary visited the tomb after the Sabbath, she first assumed that the body had been stolen. Apparently, grave robbery was common enough that a Roman emperor issued an edict decreeing it a capital offense (see the small article, "The Nazareth Inscription"). When Mary encountered an empty tomb at her first stage of faith, she, assuming the worst, and panicking, returned home and reported this information to the disciples.

The first stage of faith was practical. She arrived to complete the burial process but was not prepared for the outcome. The second stage involved various reactions to the burial clothes.

See the Clothes (20:3–15)

After "Simon Peter and the other disciple, the one Jesus loved," heard Mary's report, they ran to the tomb (John 20:2–4). Seeing Jesus' burial clothes, the disciples and Mary Magdalene reacted differently. The disciple whom Jesus loved and Peter saw the evidence first. The first disciple peered over the entrance, saw the grave clothes, and "believed" (20:8). Simon Peter followed, entered the tomb, and noticed the condition of the burial clothes. While the disciples saw, believed, and returned home, Mary remained in the garden and attempted to find evidence to support her theory of a stolen body.

The Gospel of John mentions burial clothes twice. In both cases, the reference points to the deceased's past life. When Jesus raised Lazarus from the grave in John 11:44, Lazarus came out wearing the strips of linen. Lazarus's rescue from death was temporary; he ultimately faced the reality of death. His past eventually caught up with him.

In contrast to Lazarus's situation, Jesus' clothes remained folded in the tomb. For the onlookers, the condition of Jesus' clothes was significant in two ways. First, Jesus left his burial clothes behind and conquered the grave. His past life was complete. A new dawn had begun. While the past no longer determined the present, the future invaded the present with resurrection garments. Second, the condition of the clothes answered the stolen-body question. A thief would not have taken the time to fold the cloth. Therefore, the folded napkin signaled that something miraculous had happened.

Mary returned to the tomb and saw two men sitting on either side of the place where the body was supposed to be laid. Still grieving over the loss of her teacher, Mary failed to see beyond the clothes and into the eyes of angels. When she stooped to peer into the tomb like the disciple Jesus loved, she evidently missed the brilliant experience of angels and repeated her assertion that the body was likely stolen (20:13).

Mary also missed the sound of Jesus' voice and the appearance of Jesus' resurrected body. Still focused on the conspiracy and then the clothes, she turned from the tomb and saw a man she supposed to be a gardener. Ironically, she accused Jesus of being in on the conspiracy of his stolen body (20:15).

The second stage of faith involved the mystery of incomplete belief. One disciple recognized and believed; the other did not. Neither of the disciples, however, understood the resurrection (20:9). Their reactions were significant. Despite one's belief, neither was prepared to tell the good news because resurrection did not yet accompany their belief.

Mary recognized the clothes but did not realize their significance. On the journey of grief, her sorrow overwhelmed her so much that she missed the sight of angels and the sound of Jesus' voice.

We do not know how three followers of Jesus, at this point, could still have incomplete resurrection hope. We do know that on the journey from the cemetery to home, grieving people go through a process much like Mary's and the disciples. Their journey is incomplete until they turn from the clothes of the past to the Lord of the present.

Meet the Lord (20:16–17)

To take the next step on the journey, Jesus confronted Mary in the garden with a powerful resurrection message. He began by calling her name, and she instantly recognized him. But her reaction was similar to her reaction in the second stage of grief. Wanting to hold on to the relationship she had with him in the past, she addressed him as if she was the student and he the teacher: "Rabboni" (20:16).

Jesus, however, was no longer a teacher; and he was no longer bound by the memories of the past that he shared with disciples. He wanted her to recognize him as Lord, and he reprimanded her by saying, "Do not hold onto me" (20:17).

Scholars have debated why Jesus reprimanded Mary for holding onto him. The Greek can be read as either *stop holding, stop touching, stop clinging to me,* or *stop clinging to my clothes.* In the context of the grave clothes mentioned in the tomb, the best sense of the phrase involves the clothes. Jesus invited Mary into a deeper relationship signified by turning loose of the clothes.

Mary needed to stop holding onto Jesus' garments because the clothes were symbolic of the memories of the past when Mary only knew Jesus as a teacher. He had been well known as the teacher of the first disciples (John 1). He taught Nicodemus by night (John 3). Mary wanted to have a little more time with the teacher and to hold onto those moments. Yet, Jesus was always more than a teacher, a fact confirmed by his resurrection. Mary needed to report this news to Jesus' family, and Jesus wanted to appear before the Father (20:17).

Jesus did not come back for Mary or for anyone else to hold on to the past. He did not come to say, *Let's rekindle the precious memories and remember the good old days.*

Likewise for Christians, the past is no longer the way we predict the future. Our past lives, our past mistakes, or our past roles cannot forecast our future after an encounter with Jesus. The resurrection changes how we relate to Jesus as the risen Lord and to those who surround the tomb. When resurrection occurs, the past does not repeat itself.

The resurrection of Christ invades our present and calls us to encounter Jesus as the risen Lord standing in our midst in every circumstance of life, especially the moments like Mary's when we grieve. Mary lingered long enough at the tomb to release her nostalgia for the way life used to be in order to walk forward in faith with a risen Lord changing her daily existence.

The third step of resurrection faith is just as important as the first. We release the way life used to be before we encountered the resurrected Christ. In the process of grief, nostalgia has a way of clouding our belief in Jesus as Lord. Death changes our relationships, but resurrection changes how we relate to the Lord of death and the grave. Life will never be the same from one day to the next. Resurrection, however, gives us the possibility of seeing the Lord alive in the changes of life.

Tell the News (20:18)

Mary was ready to return home a changed disciple. The first time she returned home to tell the disciples, she did not fully trust in Jesus' new identity and mission. Her second journey home was a resurrection journey. She had visited the tomb, felt the clothes, and changed her relationship with Jesus from "Teacher" to "Lord." Thus, she returned ready to take the last step of resurrection faith. Jesus sent her to share the good news with the disciples, and she became the first proclaimer of the resurrection.

According to the Gospel of John, the first disciple to believe in Jesus' resurrection did not report what he believed (20:8). Witness did not accompany belief. Mary offered, however, the first eyewitness report. Some people in the first century doubted the word of women; in contrast, the early Christians were the first to recognize the truth of their words and to follow their lead by reporting the good news.

Mary's last act was the final stage of faith. After she recognized Jesus, she told the disciples, "I have seen the Lord" (20:18).

Implication and Actions

The resurrected Christ walks with the bereaved through the process of faith in Jesus as Lord. He meets them in the cemetery and invites them on the journey to trust him and to relate to one another in new ways. Unable to return to the past, they become open to a future with him by trusting in him as Lord.

Just as Mary Magdalene journeyed from grieving student to resurrection apostle, one sent to proclaim the resurrection (20:17), so we are invited to look for the grieving and walk with them through that process. This journey lasts long after the receiving line has ended and the leftover casseroles have been eaten. It does not involve clever answers. The process requires intentional patience with loved ones on the journey. Like the disciples and Mary, sometimes the process involves incomplete belief and mistaken assumptions. But this is the journey from the cemetery to home. As faithful disciples, we contact the bereaved, walk beside them through the process, and remind them through our consistent presence that Jesus is Lord.

THE NAZARETH INSCRIPTION

The Nazareth Inscription dates from the time of Tiberius (A.D. 14–37) or Claudius (41–54).

> Ordinance of Caesar. It is my pleasure that graves and tombs remain undisturbed in perpetuity for those who have made them for the cult of their ancestors or children or members of their house. If however any man lay information that another has either demolished them, or has in any other way

extracted the buried, or has maliciously transferred them to other places in order to wrong them, or has displaced the sealing or other stones, against such a one I order that a trial be instituted, as in respect of the gods, so in regard to the cult of mortals. For it shall be much more obligatory to honour the buried. Let it be absolutely forbidden for any one to disturb them. In case of contravention I desire that the offender be sentenced to capital punishment on charge of violation of sepulture.[1]

HELPING THE GRIEVING

People who have lost a loved one tend to remember their loved one's birthday, anniversary, and date of death long after the funeral. These dates are also significant times to connect with them in a special way through a note or a card. A deacon in the church I served in San Angelo, Texas, delivered Easter lilies to widows and widowers. These gestures are the simple ways resurrection walks with a person through grief.

QUESTIONS —————————————————————————

1. Where are you on the journey from grieving student to resurrection witness?

2. How long does the journey of grief take for people following the death of loved ones?

3. What can believers do throughout the year to minister to the bereaved?

4. From your experience with grief, what actions and words should be avoided when ministering to those who have lost loved ones?

NOTES

1. C.K. Barrett, ed., *The New Testament Background: Writings from Ancient Greece and the Roman Empire*, 2d ed. (San Francisco: Harper Collins, 1987), 15

LESSON NINE

Sent to Continue Jesus' Ministry

MAIN IDEA

Jesus' command to and blessing on the disciples challenge us to allow Jesus to send us, empowered by the Holy Spirit, to live and serve as he served.

QUESTION TO EXPLORE

Where, how, and to whom does Jesus wish to send you?

STUDY AIM

To state the significance of Jesus' appearance to the disciples and to identify how I will respond to Jesus' sending and empowering *me*

QUICK READ

Jesus appeared for a second time to fearful disciples following the resurrection. He treated them like ambassadors on a mission and equipped them with the tools of the Trinity.

An American Foreign Service Officer trains to represent the country's interests abroad. The state department sends diplomats to build relationships, promote peace, handle problems, and provide a physical presence of the United States in a foreign land.[1]

Prior to resurrection, Jesus trained his disciples for an even greater mission. After the resurrection, Jesus Christ sent the disciples to represent the Trinity.

On Sunday night of Jesus' resurrection, Jesus' disciples hid fearfully. Jesus' appearance after the resurrection, however, changed the disciples from fearful followers to ambassadors sent by the Heavenly Father. He sent them in the Trinitarian power of the Father, Son, and Holy Spirit with peace, scars, and forgiveness.

JOHN 20:19–23

[19] On the evening of that first day of the week, when the disciples were together, with the doors locked for fear of the Jews, Jesus came and stood among them and said, "Peace be with you!" [20] After he said this, he showed them his hands and side. The disciples were overjoyed when they saw the Lord.

[21] Again Jesus said, "Peace be with you! As the Father has sent me, I am sending you." [22] And with that he breathed on them and said, "Receive the Holy Spirit. [23] If you forgive anyone his sins, they are forgiven; if you do not forgive them, they are not forgiven."

Peace from the Father (20:19)

The first resurrection night was no time for diplomacy. Disciples gathered "with the doors locked for fear of the Jews." They cowered in fear, aware of their reputations among their Jewish friends and their shortcomings as Jesus' followers. Jewish leadership conspired with the Romans to execute their leader, and the disciples abandoned Jesus at his moment of greatest need. Only the "disciple whom he [Jesus] loved" and some women stood near the cross (John 19:25–26). The disciples assumed they would be next to be arrested. Whether or not the Jewish leadership intended to arrest them, they had let their fears dictate their behavior.

Jesus, however, was prepared for this moment. In times of fear, God had sent his representatives to calm the people. For instance in Judges 6:23, an angel representing the Lord appeared to fearful Gideon with a greeting of peace. In the Gospel of John, a cloud of fear loomed large over the people. Generally, they were afraid of factions among the Jews. In John 7:13, Jesus' brothers did not speak openly of his whereabouts for "fear of the Jews." In John 12:42, some of the authorities believed but chose not to confess openly because of the Pharisees.

Jesus, however, had promised peace to his disciples. In John 14:27, he described a peace that came from the Father during Jesus' absence. In John 16:33, he gave them peace from the Father that accompanied them during persecution.

Just as Jesus did prior to resurrection, he brought peace to fearful disciples afterward. When they thought Jesus was absent and they were about to face persecution, Jesus fulfilled the promise of the Father's peace to them. When Jesus walked through the door on Sunday night, he embodied peace. Just as a king sent ambassadors to promote peace with another nation, so Jesus brought peace to troubled hearts of terrified followers. His action gave the same peace to disciples that God brought to Gideon centuries earlier in the Book of Judges. In the same way, the Father raised Jesus from the grave and sent him to bring peace to fearful disciples. As representatives of the Trinity, the disciples' first charge was to bring peace from the Father.

Scars of the Son (20:20–21)

Second, Jesus gave the disciples the tool of vulnerability to use as they represented the Father and the Son. He did this by showing them his scars.

With the assurance of peace from the Father (20:19), Jesus confronted the pain of the past. He revealed the places in his hands and side where he was wounded (20:20).

Jesus' scars represented his vulnerability. A community could not be formed by overlooking the consequences of painful decisions. The actions that wounded and scarred

Jesus played a part in the formation. There would be no church without crucifixion; thus, the disciples and even the Jews played a part in the process.

These scars were not trophies of pain. Rather they represented another tool the disciples could use on mission: vulnerability. If the disciples had been perfect ambassadors, they could have used different gifts. They were terribly flawed, however. They were afraid of what their families (the Jews) and their fellow believers (each other) could see in their past mistakes. They had plenty of cause for remaining in the locked room surrounded by judgment, intimidation, and fear. These disciples struggled with the darkness of the past even as they tried to live in the light of Christ.

Jesus' scars gave them permission to move on from the locked room of resurrection night as his representatives, knowing they had the presence of the Trinity. His words in John 20:21 reinforced their confidence. Just as Jesus brought peace from the Father in 20:19, Jesus greeted them with peace from Father and Son,"Peace be with you!" (20:21). He sent them from the room with his presence.

This Greek verb for *sending* can mean several things depending on the context and its use in John, and John uses this verb more than any other Gospel. In this case, Jesus used the word as an ancient king did when commissioning an ambassador to represent his interests in another country. But Jesus added a twist. In the ancient world, the king remained home and relied on the ambassador to do the work. When Jesus commissioned his disciples, he promised to go with them as they were sent. This statement can be paraphrased, *As the Father has given me the authority to go as his representative, the Father is also going with me as I go; and I am giving you the same authority to go; and we are going with you as you go.* In other words, the disciples did not go alone. The Father sent the Son and the people as representatives of the Father's message.

Jesus' words and scars indicated that the Father and the Son supported the disciples. Even when they sinned after Jesus left, they still had the guarantee of the Son's authority, protection, and vulnerability. Their actions were not excusable, but they were also not insurmountable. The disciples were not disqualified from service because of darkness in their lives.

Behind the locked doors, Jesus used failure to unite the community. These words became especially important to later Christians following their baptism. To their fellow Jews, including family members, who questioned their conversion, they could be reminded that although they continued to struggle with sin, Jesus' actions provided cover. They saw in one another the scars of the past and used those scars as a unifying force to say, *Even though we have caused problems in the past, the Father and the Son are still with us and will be despite our imperfections.*

A counselor friend says, "Don't waste your pain." Jesus used the pain of the past as a tool for the disciples to represent the Father and the Son. The last step was to share the breath of forgiveness through the Holy Spirit.

Forgiveness of the Holy Spirit (20:22–23)

The Trinitarian mission was almost complete. Jesus represented the Father's interests and had given the disciples peace and vulnerability. Next Jesus equipped them with the tool they shared with one another and the world. Through the Holy Spirit's power of forgiveness, Jesus changed how they remembered their Jewish friends and one another.

The Spirit took many forms in the New Testament. Acts 2 describes a movement like tongues of fire and like the sound of a violent wind (Acts 2:1–6). In the Gospel of John, the Spirit came in a quiet breath on a resurrection night. Jesus' breath reminded disciples of the breath of God into the first man in Genesis 2. Just as God breathed into the nostrils of Adam, so Jesus breathed the creative winds of the Spirit's forgiveness into failed disciples.[2]

As John 20:23 suggests, the disciples had a role to play when forgiveness was granted. The Spirit changed how they remembered and tracked their memories.

The disciples had no authority to grant forgiveness. Jesus granted the power to *retain sins*, or in modern terms to keep or erase a score. Prior to resurrection, the cloud of fear and failure was always in front of them. They kept

score very easily. If they continued this pattern after resurrection, they would be retaining sins. They would remind
the Jews what they did wrong, punish failed believers for
sinful problems, and generally hold the past over others'
heads.

The Holy Spirit's forgiveness after the resurrection,
however, became a creative gift from the disciples to those
very people. As representatives of the Father, Son, and
Holy Spirit, they could now remember the past differently
and retell the stories through the memory of forgiveness.
Their pain enabled them to come together. The actions of
the Jews and their friends became a part of a larger provi-
dential plan to provide the world forgiveness.

When an ambassador visits a foreign country, he or
she represents the interests of his or her home nation. The
ambassador is also familiar with the history of the relationship. Carrying memories of the past, good and bad,
the ambassador has the choice to use those memories as
a weapon of retribution or a tool to build relationships.
The ambassador can use the pain of the past to affect the
future negatively; or the ambassador can build on that
pain as a lesson to be learned for the future. The ambassador has the power to use the pain as a weapon or as a
resource.

Because the disciples were forgiven, the pain of the past
became a resource. As humans, they could not forget the
past but could remember differently. Keeping score and
reminding their friends, family, or nation of how they had

failed were no longer needed. Otherwise, such behavior would be *retaining sins*.

Because of this resurrection appearance of Jesus, the disciples became representatives of King Jesus. He did not keep score, and he saw the past as a pathway to a relationship given through the creative breath of the Holy Spirit's forgiveness. As they went to friends, fellow Jews, and failed believers, they were given the power to wipe the past scores clean.

As humans, we cannot forgive and forget completely. But with God's power of forgiveness, we can change what we remember. Prior to forgiveness, we remember what we have done wrong, the pain that others have inflicted, the open wounds, and the regrets. With the breath of forgiveness, we become agents of different memories. We remember how God used the problems of the past by Jesus' bringing us together in the midst of pain. We remember that we were re-created by God behind the doors of fear. As the Christian author and professor Lewis Smedes said, "Forgiving does not erase the bitter past. A healed memory is not a deleted memory. Forgiving what we cannot forget creates a new way to remember."[3]

Applying to Life

Jesus appeared to the disciples in John 20 to equip them with the tools they needed to go to the people they knew and feared the most: their fellow Jews and other failed disciples. Those groups today represent our families of origin, friends, and believers who question our commitment. The same Pharisees and other Jews who intimidated the disciples grew up beside them in Capernaum. Knowing them well, they were also some of the first to change their lives after the disciples shared their faith.

In the same way, friends and family know our churches and our lives better than others do. They have carried with them the memories, pain, and scars of the past. We have a Trinitarian mission, and Jesus gives us the tools as ambassadors in our most familiar relationships.

Like diplomats on a mission for a head of state, we are sent to represent the Trinity's interests and represent what the Trinity looks like through our lives. To do so, we, as Jesus' ambassadors, need the tools of the Trinity: peace, vulnerability, and forgiveness. Through these tools, God breathes life again into our significant relationships.

BELIEVING JEWS

Jews in the Gospel of John appear to be responsible for many problems, but they cannot be lumped into one group. The Gospel of John records episodes of believing Jews (Nicodemus, Joseph of Arimathea) and unbelieving Gentiles (Herod, Pilate).

As Gentiles were diverse, so Jews were a diverse group. At least five different Jewish religious parties existed in Jesus' day: Pharisees, Sadducees, Essenes, Herodians, and Zealots. Few of them could agree on matters of Jewish law or preferences. The Sanhedrin that met by night during Jesus' trial was just a small cluster of religious leadership.

The Gospel of John is not anti-Semitic. All people share a responsibility in Jesus' death. Furthermore, without Jewish families, Christianity would not exist. Formed out of networks with other Jewish people within synagogues and homes, the church eventually spread to Gentiles.

SPIRITUAL FORMATION

Resurrection invites us out of our individualistic world into the company of friends who can share the burdens of life and help us recover resurrection light. This is a process called spiritual formation. Instead of a program of growth where the goals are never-ending, resurrection forms us into community.

Find a companion on the resurrection journey with whom you can be honest. Admit your faults, and share the joy of a clean slate. Wherever "two or three" are gathered, the Spirit is breathing forgiveness among them.

QUESTIONS

1. What are the scars of the past caused by friends and family that affect your relationships with them?

2. How do you relate to the concept that one does not *forgive and forget* but rather *remembers differently*? What good events have come out of painful memories?

3. What difference does it make in this passage that Jesus appears in the power of the Trinity?

4. What is the difference between peace that is given from the Father and peace that is achieved through human conquest?

5. How does a believer balance being vulnerable in community with sharing *way too much information*?

NOTES

1. http://www.usaid.gov/careers/fsofaq.html. Accessed 10/19/10.

2. Eugene Peterson, *Living the Resurrection: the Risen Christ in Everyday Life* (Colorado Springs, CO: NavPress, 2006), 109.

3. Lewis Smedes, *The Art of Forgiving: When You Need to Forgive and Don't Know How* (New York: Ballantine Books, 1996), 171.

FOCAL TEXT
John 20:24–31

BACKGROUND
John 11:16; 14:5; 20:24–31

LESSON TEN

Confessing Who Jesus Is

MAIN IDEA

Jesus' resurrection appearance that led to Thomas's confession of faith calls us to confess our faith in Jesus as our Lord and God and to encourage friends who are skeptics.

QUESTION TO EXPLORE

Are you insisting that Jesus do anything else so that you will confess, "My Lord and my God," and live your confession?

STUDY AIM

To affirm my faith in Jesus as Lord and God and to identify ways of encouraging someone who is skeptical about the gospel to believe

QUICK READ

Although present for much of Jesus' ministry, Thomas missed the most important moment. When Jesus appeared after the resurrection, he showed us how and where to find people who have missed the resurrection life.

The class gathers for the final exam before graduation. With one week left until commencement, the seniors know that all they really need to do is show up and they can graduate. The teacher calls the roll. Everyone is present except one who needs to take the test to finish. When everyone has finished the exam, the teacher decides to drive to the student's home. The door is locked; the lights are off. Something has happened, and the teacher wonders what to do next. Does the teacher let the student miss one of the greatest chances of his life?

Perhaps Jesus faced a similar choice with one of his disciples. Thomas had been with him throughout his ministry but had missed the important appearance to the disciples. When Jesus appeared to him through a door locked by fear and skepticism, Jesus gave the kind of evidence needed to encourage someone who is skeptical about the gospel to believe.

JOHN 20:24–31

24 Now Thomas (called Didymus), one of the Twelve, was not with the disciples when Jesus came. **25** So the other disciples told him, "We have seen the Lord!"

But he said to them, "Unless I see the nail marks in his hands and put my finger where the nails were, and put my hand into his side, I will not believe it."

26 A week later his disciples were in the house again, and Thomas was with them. Though the doors were locked, Jesus came and stood among them and said, "Peace be with you!" **27** Then he said to Thomas, "Put your finger here; see my hands. Reach out your hand and put it into my side. Stop doubting and believe."

28 Thomas said to him, "My Lord and my God!"

29 Then Jesus told him, "Because you have seen me, you have believed; blessed are those who have not seen and yet have believed."

30 Jesus did many other miraculous signs in the presence of his disciples, which are not recorded in this book. **31** But these are written that you may believe that Jesus is the Christ, the Son of God, and that by believing you may have life in his name.

Missing People

In the Gospel of John, Jesus visited people who missed the Jewish forms of worship. They struggled with belief, and Jesus challenged them in unique ways.

For instance, in John 4, Jesus met a Samaritan woman at a public well. She filled the void left by religion with her relationships with five different husbands. As a Samaritan, she did not worship at the Jewish temple; she worshiped on Mount Gerizim. Even if she could have worshiped in the temple, her moral life was a failure. She longed for a drink of water and was skeptical at first about the kind of man Jesus was. Yet Jesus satisfied her thirst by pointing her toward worship "in spirit and truth," worship of Jesus Christ standing in front of her (John 4:24).

In John 5, Jesus encountered at the local healing pool another man absent from Jewish worship. He was paralyzed physically, mentally, and spiritually. As a lame man, he could not get into the pool of Bethesda when the waters were stirred. Mentally he had become a victim of his own circumstances. When first engaged in conversation with Jesus, he was skeptical about his circumstances and announced, "I have no one to help me" (John 5:7). Spiritually, he could not worship in the temple because of his physical condition. He was missing out on the abundant life Jesus promised (10:10).

Jesus cut through his conditions with a penetrating question (5:6), "Do you want to get well?" The man chose to accept the challenge of living well and rose to new life.

The Samaritan woman and the paralytic represented the kind of prospects Jesus identified as future followers. They were missing from Jewish worship because of their choices as well as their circumstances. They were skeptical about Jesus; but when given the opportunity, they responded with hands-on participation. The Samaritan woman received a drink and told her family. The paralytic picked up his mat and walked. They were absent from traditional forms of religion, but Jesus found them.

A Missing Disciple

Prior to the resurrection, Thomas had followed Jesus and was even willing to rush into a sacrificial role if necessary. With reckless abandon, he announced he would follow him to the cross (11:16). Yet his reaction to Jesus revealed his impertinence. In John 14:5, Thomas asked for clarification about where Jesus was going, but little more is known about his depth of faith until after the resurrection.

We do know, however, that Thomas was missing. Like most of the disciples, he was not present at the cross. He did not go to the garden tomb to anoint Jesus' body; only Mary Magdalene did. On Sunday night, he was not present with the disciples when Jesus appeared to them in the locked room.

Thomas, often branded as the doubter or the skeptic, was not where he needed to be. In this case, he was apparently overcome with the same grief and fear of the disciples described in 20:19–23. His reaction led him to greater uncertainty. Rather than joining with his friends, he remained skeptical. He had become like the Samaritan woman and the paralytic whom Jesus encountered earlier in the Gospel of John. Thomas needed Jesus' personal attention.

A Present Lord (20:24–28)

One week after Jesus' first appearance to the disciples, he appeared to the missing disciple in much the same way. The disciples were behind the locked door; and despite their testimony to their friend, Thomas remained unconvinced.

Jesus presented himself in two ways. To the disciples who had already seen and heard him, he repeated the experience of the previous week. He arrived through the door and greeted them with the Jewish greeting of peace.

To the missing disciple, Jesus gestured and invited Thomas to look at his hands and touch his side (20:27). We are not sure whether Thomas accepted the offer. I imagine the gesture is all that Thomas needed. Jesus' movement was like a sign pointing the way to belief. When he extended his hands, he confirmed what Thomas had missed all along. Thomas's skepticism was overcome. He confessed unequivocal belief in Jesus' divine nature to his friends and to his Savior: "My Lord and my God" (20:28).

Some followers needed more than appearances and greetings. They required more than showing up and attending the faith; they wanted hands-on participation in the experience. The Samaritan woman, the paralytic, and Thomas were the kinds of followers Jesus personally sought in order to give them such hands-on experience.

The Samaritan woman provided Jesus something to drink; the paralytic picked up his mat and walked. Thomas needed to experience Jesus.

Seeing and Believing Disciples (20:29–31)

Disciples came to believe in Jesus in two ways in the Gospel of John: (1) the personal encounter in which Jesus directly sought them and (2) the testimony of others who repeated the story. Jesus affirmed both kinds of faith.

For the missing, the old saying is true: *Seeing is believing.* They came to faith when Jesus encountered them personally. The only way the Samaritan woman, the paralytic, and Thomas would believe was for Jesus to give them enough evidence to follow.

For other disciples, the testimony of others was enough. Jesus blessed those for whom *believing is seeing.* They believed without the physical encounter. This resurrection appearance became a bridge to generations of followers who never saw Jesus physically but believed what generations have said ever since the resurrection, "We have seen the Lord" (20:25).

Belief in Jesus because of physical experience or because of the testimony of others generates the same response. Followers demonstrate that Jesus is Lord through their lives. The Samaritan woman changed her life and told her family and friends. The paralytic picked up his mat and walked. Thomas, who had demonstrated impertinence, overcame skepticism with a new orientation to Christ.

John 20:30–31 states the bottom line in discipleship throughout the Gospel of John. How a disciple comes to believe in Jesus is not nearly as important as the effect that belief has on the disciple's life. According to John, belief in Jesus equals a complete life change around one who is the "Christ, the Son of God," a change that creates a new "life in his name."

Both the missing and the present disciples had new lifestyles once they believed in Jesus. Belief was a full-bodied, hands-on response. Just as the Samaritan woman, the paralytic, Thomas, and the other disciples were different after they encountered Jesus, these believing disciples experienced a new kind of life. They re-oriented their lives around their "Lord and God." Their vocations, occupations, and careers changed because they experienced first-hand what seeing and believing mean.

Applying to Life

We can encourage skeptics about the gospel through a life worth seeing and believing. We represent the life and evidence of Christ to them through our lives. The most important evidence a skeptic needs is to see a life that demonstrates the confession, *Jesus is my Lord and my God*. As we live out the confession, we go to the people who by circumstance or choice are missing from worship but who still desire living water, physical healing, or personal evidence in their lives.

Jesus found the Samaritan woman at a public watering spot. He found the paralytic at the place where people needed healing physically. He found Thomas behind a locked door of skepticism.

Where do *we* find them? These are the friends we drink coffee with and the neighbors we visit in the hospital. We encounter the missing frequently. In each place, we are invited to engage them with a life that demonstrates the difference a risen Lord makes and to give them enough evidence to overcome their skepticism.

WHO'S MISSING?

Thomas was the kind of believer who followed Jesus to the upper room but needed another personal encounter after resurrection. He reminds me of college students who grew up in church, followed their parents' faith through adolescence, but need to reinforce belief and commitment during and after college. Scholars estimate that 75% of young men and women leave the church between ages 16–24, and 40% leave by age 35. Of those who return to church, 30% go to other denominations.[1] People in this age group, including college students, have always been missing from church, but now the problem is epidemic.

The church might classify them as *lost*, but Jesus treats them as missing.[2] Social media offers us a chance to reach out. Most of the missing can be located through Facebook® and Twitter®. By starting virtual conversations, we gain access into the personal world of the missing and develop a way to create personal conversations built through relationships. A brief comment on the internet can lead to meaningful conversation at a coffee shop if we look for the missing.

WHAT TO DO?

Fred and Mike played golf in the same foursome for years. Fred always knew Mike was a believer. They never scheduled a round on Sunday morning, but Mike never invited Fred to church.

When Fred was diagnosed with brain cancer, Mike decided to visit him in the hospital. Before he went, he realized that faith had never been a topic of conversation on the golf course. They abided by the custom of not talking about politics or religion, but Mike was now ashamed that he had never brought up his faith.

When Mike visits Fred in the hospital, what should he do? Should he offer to pray with Fred at the bedside?

QUESTIONS

1. How does believing that Jesus is "my Lord and my God" affect your life?

2. What causes a person to become skeptical about belief in Jesus?

3. What causes a person to drop out of church and become missing?

4. Where do you encounter the missing in your world today? How can you engage them in the life of Christ?

NOTES

1. Roland Martinson, "Spiritual But Not Religious: Reaching an Invisible Generation," *Currents in Theology and Mission* 29.5 (October 2002): 326 (15).

2. Jim Henderson, *Evangelism without Additives*, 2d ed. (Colorado Springs: WaterBrook, 2007), 17.

LESSON ELEVEN
*Follow Jesus—
No Excuses*

MAIN IDEA

Jesus' questioning Peter at the breakfast appearance indicates that no matter what has happened in the past, what the situation in the present, or what someone else does, we are to follow Jesus fully.

QUESTION TO EXPLORE

Are you letting something in your past, your present, or your relationship with another person keep you from following Jesus?

STUDY AIM

To trace the flow of Jesus' conversation with Peter and to decide to respond to Jesus' call to follow him, whether in first-time faith or fullness of service

QUICK READ

Jesus appeared at the workplace to disciples who had returned to their jobs. This breakfast on the beach offered Peter a chance to deepen his love relationship with his Lord.

On special Saturday mornings when I was a child, my family had a tradition. We woke up early to enjoy breakfast on the picnic tables overlooking Pensacola Bay. We loaded the Coleman® cook stove; my mother fried the bacon; and my dad and I fished off the pier. We watched the sun rise over the horizon. I can still smell the scrambled eggs. This tradition of love is one that I remember to this day.

Jesus and his disciples shared special moments on the beach—not as a family meeting place but as the office workplace. Early one morning, Jesus met them and taught his lead disciple the kind of resurrection love he needed for the rest of his life.

JOHN 21:1–23

1 Afterward Jesus appeared again to his disciples, by the Sea of Tiberias. It happened this way: **2** Simon Peter, Thomas (called Didymus), Nathanael from Cana in Galilee, the sons of Zebedee, and two other disciples were together. **3** "I'm going out to fish," Simon Peter told them, and they said, "We'll go with you." So they went out and got into the boat, but that night they caught nothing.

4 Early in the morning, Jesus stood on the shore, but the disciples did not realize that it was Jesus.

5 He called out to them, "Friends, haven't you any fish?"

"No," they answered.

6 He said, "Throw your net on the right side of the boat and you will find some." When they did, they were unable to haul the net in because of the large number of fish.

7 Then the disciple whom Jesus loved said to Peter, "It is the Lord!" As soon as Simon Peter heard him say, "It is the Lord," he wrapped his outer garment around him (for he had taken it off) and jumped into the water. **8** The other disciples followed in the boat, towing the net full of fish, for they were not far from shore, about a hundred yards. **9** When they landed, they saw a fire of burning coals there with fish on it, and some bread.

10 Jesus said to them, "Bring some of the fish you have just caught."

11 Simon Peter climbed aboard and dragged the net ashore. It was full of large fish, 153, but even with so many the net was not torn. **12** Jesus said to them, "Come and have breakfast." None of the disciples dared ask him, "Who are you?" They knew it was the Lord. **13** Jesus came, took the bread and gave it to them, and did the same with the fish. **14** This was now the third time Jesus appeared to his disciples after he was raised from the dead.

15 When they had finished eating, Jesus said to Simon Peter, "Simon son of John, do you truly love me more than these?"

"Yes, Lord," he said, "you know that I love you."

Jesus said, "Feed my lambs."

16 Again Jesus said, "Simon son of John, do you truly love me?"

He answered, "Yes, Lord, you know that I love you."

Jesus said, "Take care of my sheep."

17 The third time he said to him, "Simon son of John, do you love me?"

Peter was hurt because Jesus asked him the third time, "Do you love me?" He said, "Lord, you know all things; you know that I love you."

Jesus said, "Feed my sheep. **18** I tell you the truth, when you were younger you dressed yourself and went where you wanted; but when you are old you will stretch out your hands, and someone else will dress you and lead you where you do not want to go." **19** Jesus said this to indicate the kind of death by which Peter would glorify God. Then he said to him, "Follow me!"

20 Peter turned and saw that the disciple whom Jesus loved was following them. (This was the one who had leaned back against Jesus at the supper and had said, "Lord, who is going to betray you?") **21** When Peter saw him, he asked, "Lord, what about him?"

22 Jesus answered, "If I want him to remain alive until I return, what is that to you? You must follow me." **23** Because of this, the rumor spread among the brothers that this disciple would not die. But Jesus did not say that he would not die; he only said, "If I want him to remain alive until I return, what is that to you?"

Back to Work (21:1–14)

The Gospel of John opens with the Word becoming flesh and moving into the neighborhood (John 1:14). During one of John the Baptist's sermons, Jesus called the first two disciples: Andrew and his brother Simon Peter (1:40). The Gospel ends with the Word working on the job with one of those first disciples, Simon Peter. Jesus met Peter on the beach of the "Sea of Tiberias," the Roman name for the Sea of Galilee. The Sea of Galilee is the small lake on the northern edge of ancient Israel that feeds the Jordan River and supplies water to this region.

The beach was the office for Peter and six other disciples who had followed Jesus through the Fourth Gospel. They were also business associates and maybe even competitors trying to make a living through a new way of life after the resurrection.

Now pictured as a place for sunbathing and resort living, the beach of Jesus' day was a place for making a living the hard way. Poor fishermen rowed boats no longer than fifteen feet long in the lake and set dragnets that could be pulled onto the shore. For security and stability of the nets, the fishermen monitored them by remaining in the water throughout the night. Dressed in what was likely just loin cloths, the workers came ashore around sunrise, stood on either end of the dragnet, and pulled their catch ashore.

The miraculous catch was familiar to the disciples. They had seen Jesus' miracles before, and this time they recognized Jesus after the miracle occurred (21:7).

Notice that Jesus valued their work to the point of participating in it himself. They were doing their work with Christ.

Back to the Flock (21:15–17)

To continue their work as disciples, Jesus needed to restore a relationship with Peter, who had denied him three times (18:15–18, 25–27). Jesus restored Peter by delegating his role as the Good Shepherd to Peter as another shepherd of God's flock.

Jesus first used the shepherd imagery in John 10. He compared his life to a shepherd who lay at the entrance of a sheep gate. The shepherd's body served a two-fold purpose: to keep the sheep inside and to alert the shepherd if someone tried to steal or attack the flock through the opening in the fence. The point was clear in a simple metaphor. The shepherd was prepared to do whatever was necessary and in the best interest of the sheep to protect them.

Jesus prepared Peter for the work Peter was about to do. Much like the shepherd who gave his life for the sheep, Peter needed to be prepared to do what was in the sheep's best interest. People are like sheep in that they do not naturally follow shepherds but other sheep. Peter's role would depend on his ability as the leader of God's flock. Peter needed to love the Good Shepherd even more than he loved the sheep and to guide the sheep to the Good Shepherd.

To give Peter this role, Jesus brought him back to the flock. He began with Peter in the role he knew best, as a fisherman. Stripped for work (21:7), Peter likely had just one set of clothes. Jesus received him just as he was.

On the beach, Jesus restored him with three questions. The setting of charcoal was reminiscent of the charcoal campfire in Caiaphas's courtyard. Jesus knew Peter could not take on a new role as shepherd without facing the past and surrendering its effect on his life. Peter had to forgive himself so his regret would not have control over his future. Peter came to Jesus *just as he was*, but Jesus did not want him to remain in that condition for long.

Jesus asked Peter three pivotal questions paralleling the three denials of Peter (13:38; 18:17, 25–27). The Greek words for "love" in John 21:15–17 differ, but the effect is the same. The point was not which kind of love as defined in the dictionary. The point of the questions was the slow, intense restoration of the lead disciple into a place of service and sacrifice. Jesus' love was not just for Jesus' or Peter's sake, but for the sake of the sheep Jesus was entrusting to his disciple.

We might come to Jesus "Just as I Am," as the gospel song states, but Jesus does not want to leave us just as we always were. He begins a process of change in a love relationship as we fall in love again. The gateway to surrender is resurrected love, rising out of the charcoal ashes of life and inviting us to be resurrected. Resurrection forces us to confront issues we would have rather simply ignored. Instead, we face our frailties, surrender the effect on our lives, and move forward in a love relationship reoriented around the call of Christ in our lives.

Just as a love relationship changes our priorities, values, location, proximity, and commitments, so Peter's relationship with Jesus changed and deepened with each question. How many times does it take for someone to ask whether you love him or her? Peter needed to be asked at least three times to prepare himself to go forward.

Back to the Future (21:18–23)

Following his restoration, Jesus brought Peter's future into the present. Throughout his life, Peter had freedom to choose his occupation. From then on, he prepared for the ultimate sacrifice. Peter's life paralleled Jesus' life. Peter became a model of sacrifice to the other disciples when someone else would take him where he did not want to go.

In speculating about the future, most people want to know not only their destiny but also that of others. The same was true for Peter. He reacted to the anticipation of the end by asking about the beloved disciple. Jesus explained carefully that their destinies were not con-trolled by predictions. They were not to worry about the time or circumstances when Jesus returned. As shepherds of the flock, they served the same purpose as the Good Shepherd, whom they loved: to supply the flock whatever was needed to "Follow Jesus."

The resurrection changed Peter's view of the future. No longer was he tied to his job as a fisherman but neither was he guaranteed an easy life. He was not even given the privilege of comparing his life with another disciple's. In the same way, the resurrection changes how we understand the future. Instead of the future being a pathway toward achievement, or a place where we plan for retirement, or a distant mountain we will one day climb, the future is now. The future that was seemingly a long way off has invaded the present. And that future is Jesus' resurrection. Just as Jesus was resurrected from the dead, believers are promised the same after we die. So, whether we like Peter give our lives for the sheep or like the beloved disciple have other tasks, we live as if today is resurrection day. We live to do what is in the best interests of the sheep every day.

No one knows the future, but the love we have for Christ and his love for us guides our faithfulness. We approach the present like a good shepherd laying down his life for his sheep.

In doing so, we recognize that some people have been designated overseers of the flock while others are one of the sheep. Each person, however, follows Jesus. The call to follow happens in first-time faith in the Good Shepherd when we answer the question, "Do you love me?" We also give our lives more fully in service in response to a deepening love relationship with Christ. That commitment might result in a change at work. As Peter moved from fisherman to shepherd, so our occupations might change.

Our vocations, however, are always the same: living out a calling as resurrected believers.

Fishermen, shepherds, and all God's workers share the same circumstances. When we surrender to Christ in the midst of our daily routine, we follow him into a future that comes into full view through love for him.

Implications and Actions

For most people, an encounter with Christ's resurrection love does not send them to an exotic location or to a seminary. Christ sends us back to work to live out resurrection love around the people who know us best, warts and all. The workplace has a way of knowing us at our best and worst. Jesus begins there. Our work reveals our capacity for unity with other believers and with Jesus. The church is at her best when believers work together on missions. Believers are at their best when they take Jesus' mission with them to the workplace.

Jesus blesses our work with his presence and invites us to trust him with our career goals, dreams, and ambitions. He cares about the fish, all 153 of them. He begins at work because he invites us to sacrifice for those whom we work with, care for, and see every day.

In an environment of competitiveness, layoffs, and gossip, we live the resurrection. Out of resurrection love, we do what is in the best interest of the sheep. No matter what the future holds, we are compelled by resurrection love to sacrifice our interests for the good of God's flock.

LIVING THE RESURRECTION TOGETHER

If we watched a 3-D movie of Jesus on an IMAX screen with the benefit of glasses, we could watch images jump off the screen and into our laps. The resurrection accounts in the Gospel of John add another dimension to the experience. Through John's lenses, the disciples not only saw Jesus come alive before their eyes (3-D), but they experienced that belief together with one another (4-D). Belief was more than checking a box at the bottom of a card indicating that a person agreed with what they heard. In this Gospel, one's life reflected belief. The two were inseparable. Belief and action went together. A Samaritan woman tells her family. A paralytic takes up a mat and walks. A skeptical disciple confesses, "My Lord and my God." A disciple who denied Jesus follows him all the way to his destiny of sacrifice. In each case, the believer found a community of resurrection friends to accompany him or her. Spirituality and commitment were united.

One cannot have a private faith without a public commitment together with others. The disciples needed one another to carry out the mission. As they continued Jesus' mission, the church shined resurrection light in the darkness and lived the resurrection together.

DO YOU?

Imagine the conversation between Jesus and Peter in John 21:15–17 as one between parent and child. Read the verses aloud, emphasizing different words: "Do *you* love me? Do you love *me*? Do you *love* me?" How do changes in vocal inflection and emphasis affect interpretation?

QUESTIONS

1. What circumstances or people in the past are keeping you from following Jesus?

2. How does God meet you at work? Whether you receive a paycheck or have unpaid responsibilities, how does God reveal himself on the beach of life?

3. Shepherds do what is in the best interests of their sheep. Who are the sheep under your care? What do they need from you?

4. If you were to follow Jesus fully, what's the next step you need to take to show Jesus you love him?

Our Next New Study

(Available for use beginning May 22, 2011)

PROFILES IN CHARACTER: From the Exodus Through the Return from Exile

Additional Future Adult Study

The Corinthian   For use beginning
Letters   September 2011

How to Order More Bible Study Materials

It's easy! Just fill in the following information. For additional Bible study materials available both in print and online, see www.baptistwaypress.org, or get a complete order form of available print materials—including Spanish materials—by calling 1-866-249-1799 or e-mailing baptistway@texasbaptists.org.

Title of item	Price	Quantity	Cost
This Issue:			
The Gospel of John: Light Overcoming Darkness, Part Two—Study Guide (BWP001109)	$3.55	_____	_____
The Gospel of John: Light Overcoming Darkness, Part Two—Large Print Study Guide (BWP001110)	$3.95	_____	_____
The Gospel of John: Light Overcoming Darkness, Part Two—Teaching Guide (BWP001111)	$4.50	_____	_____
Additional Issues Available:			
Growing Together in Christ—Study Guide (BWP001036)	$3.25	_____	_____
Growing Together in Christ—Teaching Guide (BWP001038)	$3.75	_____	_____
Living Faith in Daily Life—Study Guide (BWP001095)	$3.55	_____	_____
Living Faith in Daily Life—Large Print Study Guide (BWP001096)	$3.95	_____	_____
Living Faith in Daily Life—Teaching Guide (BWP001097)	$4.25	_____	_____
Participating in God's Mission—Study Guide (BWP001077)	$3.55	_____	_____
Participating in God's Mission—Large Print Study Guide (BWP001078)	$3.95	_____	_____
Participating in God's Mission—Teaching Guide (BWP001079)	$3.95	_____	_____
Genesis: People Relating to God—Study Guide (BWP001088)	$2.35	_____	_____
Genesis: People Relating to God—Large Print Study Guide (BWP001089)	$2.75	_____	_____
Genesis: People Relating to God—Teaching Guide (BWP001090)	$2.95	_____	_____
Genesis 12—50: Family Matters—Study Guide (BWP000034)	$1.95	_____	_____
Genesis 12—50: Family Matters—Teaching Guide (BWP000035)	$2.45	_____	_____
Leviticus, Numbers, Deuteronomy—Study Guide (BWP000053)	$2.35	_____	_____
Leviticus, Numbers, Deuteronomy—Large Print Study Guide (BWP000052)	$2.35	_____	_____
Leviticus, Numbers, Deuteronomy—Teaching Guide (BWP000054)	$2.95	_____	_____
1 and 2 Samuel—Study Guide (BWP000002)	$2.35	_____	_____
1 and 2 Samuel—Large Print Study Guide (BWP000001)	$2.35	_____	_____
1 and 2 Samuel—Teaching Guide (BWP000003)	$2.95	_____	_____
1 and 2 Kings: Leaders and Followers—Study Guide (BWP001025)	$2.95	_____	_____
1 and 2 Kings: Leaders and Followers Large Print Study Guide (BWP001026)	$3.15	_____	_____
1 and 2 Kings: Leaders and Followers Teaching Guide (BWP001027)	$3.45	_____	_____
Ezra, Haggai, Zechariah, Nehemiah, Malachi—Study Guide (BWP001071)	$3.25	_____	_____
Ezra, Haggai, Zechariah, Nehemiah, Malachi—Large Print Study Guide (BWP001072)	$3.55	_____	_____
Ezra, Haggai, Zechariah, Nehemiah, Malachi—Teaching Guide (BWP001073)	$3.75	_____	_____
Job, Ecclesiastes, Habakkuk, Lamentations—Study Guide (BWP001016)	$2.75	_____	_____
Job, Ecclesiastes, Habakkuk, Lamentations—Large Print Study Guide (BWP001017)	$2.85	_____	_____
Job, Ecclesiastes, Habakkuk, Lamentations—Teaching Guide (BWP001018)	$3.25	_____	_____
Psalms and Proverbs—Study Guide (BWP001000)	$2.75	_____	_____
Psalms and Proverbs—Teaching Guide (BWP001002)	$3.25	_____	_____
Matthew: Hope in the Resurrected Christ—Study Guide (BWP001066)	$3.25	_____	_____
Matthew: Hope in the Resurrected Christ—Large Print Study Guide (BWP001067)	$3.55	_____	_____
Matthew: Hope in the Resurrected Christ—Teaching Guide (BWP001068)	$3.75	_____	_____
Mark: Jesus' Works and Words—Study Guide (BWP001022)	$2.95	_____	_____
Mark: Jesus' Works and Words—Large Print Study Guide (BWP001023)	$3.15	_____	_____
Mark:Jesus' Works and Words—Teaching Guide (BWP001024)	$3.45	_____	_____
Jesus in the Gospel of Mark—Study Guide (BWP000066)	$1.95	_____	_____
Jesus in the Gospel of Mark—Teaching Guide (BWP000067)	$2.45	_____	_____
Luke: Journeying to the Cross—Study Guide (BWP000057)	$2.35	_____	_____
Luke: Journeying to the Cross—Large Print Study Guide (BWP000056)	$2.35	_____	_____
Luke: Journeying to the Cross—Teaching Guide (BWP000058)	$2.95	_____	_____
The Gospel of John: Light Overcoming Darkness, Part One—Study Guide (BWP001104)	$3.55	_____	_____
The Gospel of John: Light Overcoming Darkness, Part One—Large Print Study Guide (BWP001105)	$3.95	_____	_____
The Gospel of John: Light Overcoming Darkness, Part One—Teaching Guide (BWP001106)	$4.50	_____	_____
The Gospel of John: The Word Became Flesh—Study Guide (BWP001008)	$2.75	_____	_____
The Gospel of John: The Word Became Flesh—Large Print Study Guide (BWP001009)	$2.85	_____	_____
The Gospel of John: The Word Became Flesh—Teaching Guide (BWP001010)	$3.25	_____	_____
Acts: Toward Being a Missional Church—Study Guide (BWP001013)	$2.75	_____	_____
Acts: Toward Being a Missional Church—Large Print Study Guide (BWP001014)	$2.85	_____	_____
Acts: Toward Being a Missional Church—Teaching Guide (BWP001015)	$3.25	_____	_____

Item	Price		
Romans: What God Is Up To—Study Guide (BWP001019)	$2.95	_____	_____
Romans: What God Is Up To—Large Print Study Guide (BWP001020)	$3.15	_____	_____
Romans: What God Is Up To—Teaching Guide (BWP001021)	$3.45	_____	_____
Galatians and 1&2 Thessalonians—Study Guide (BWP001080)	$3.55	_____	_____
Galatians and 1&2 Thessalonians—Large Print Study Guide (BWP001081)	$3.95	_____	_____
Galatians and 1&2 Thessalonians—Teaching Guide (BWP001082)	$3.95	_____	_____
Ephesians, Philippians, Colossians—Study Guide (BWP001060)	$3.25	_____	_____
Ephesians, Philippians, Colossians—Large Print Study Guide (BWP001061)	$3.55	_____	_____
Ephesians, Philippians, Colossians—Teaching Guide (BWP001062)	$3.75	_____	_____
1, 2 Timothy, Titus, Philemon—Study Guide (BWP000092)	$2.75	_____	_____
1, 2 Timothy, Titus, Philemon—Large Print Study Guide (BWP000091)	$2.85	_____	_____
1, 2 Timothy, Titus, Philemon—Teaching Guide (BWP000093)	$3.25	_____	_____
Letters of James and John—Study Guide (BWP001101)	$3.55	_____	_____
Letters of James and John—Large Print Study Guide (BWP001102)	$3.95	_____	_____
Letters of James and John—Teaching Guide (BWP001103)	$4.25	_____	_____
Revelation—Study Guide (BWP000084)	$2.35	_____	_____
Revelation—Large Print Study Guide (BWP000083)	$2.35	_____	_____
Revelation—Teaching Guide (BWP000085)	$2.95	_____	_____

Coming for use beginning May 22, 2011

Item	Price		
Profiles in Character—Study Guide (BWP001112)	$3.55	_____	_____
Profiles in Character—Large Print Study Guide (BWP001113)	$4.25	_____	_____
Profiles in Character—Teaching Guide (BWP001114)	$4.95	_____	_____

Standard (UPS/Mail) Shipping Charges*			
Order Value	Shipping charge**	Order Value	Shipping charge**
$.01—$9.99	$6.50	$160.00—$199.99	$22.00
$10.00—$19.99	$8.00	$200.00—$249.99	$26.00
$20.00—$39.99	$9.00	$250.00—$299.99	$28.00
$40.00—$59.99	$10.00	$300.00—$349.99	$32.00
$60.00—$79.99	$11.00	$350.00—$399.99	$40.00
$80.00—$99.99	$12.00	$400.00—$499.99	$48.00
$100.00—$129.99	$14.00	$500.00—$599.99	$58.00
$130.00—$159.99	$18.00	$600.00—$799.99	$70.00**

Cost
of items (Order value) _____

Shipping charges
(see chart*) _____

TOTAL _____

*Plus, applicable taxes for individuals and other taxable entities (not churches) within Texas will be added. Please call 1-866-249-1799 if the exact amount is needed prior to ordering.

**For order values $800.00 and above, please call 1-866-249-1799 or check www.baptistwaypress.org

Please allow three weeks for standard delivery. For express shipping service: Call 1-866-249-1799 for information on additional charges.

YOUR NAME _____

PHONE _____

YOUR CHURCH _____

DATE ORDERED _____

SHIPPING ADDRESS _____

CITY _____

STATE _____ ZIP CODE _____

E-MAIL _____

MAIL this form with your check for the total amount to
BAPTISTWAY PRESS, Baptist General Convention of Texas,
333 North Washington, Dallas, TX 75246-1798
(Make checks to "Baptist Executive Board.")

OR, **FAX** your order anytime to: 214-828-5376, and we will bill you.

OR, **CALL** your order toll-free: 1-866-249-1799
(M-Fri 8:30 a.m.-5:00 p.m. central time), and we will bill you.

OR, **E-MAIL** your order to our internet e-mail address:
baptistway@texasbaptists.org, and we will bill you.

OR, **ORDER ONLINE** at www.baptistwaypress.org.

We look forward to receiving your order! Thank you!